One Man's Treasure

Colin's Collection

A LUTON MISCELLANY

Edited by Georgina Cook

In Memory of Local Historian Colin R Cook

Author of "The Story of Limbury-cum-Biscot"

This book is dedicated to my sons Peter and Derek in memory of their Father Colin R Cook 1936 - 2007

First published October 2012 by Cook Family Publishing

ISBN 978-0-9557010-1-6
Designed and typeset by Moren Associates Limited
www.morenassociates.co.uk

Printed in Great Britain by TJ International, Padstow, Cornwall

Front cover picture: Colin with his beloved Austin Ruby and some of his Collector's items. Picture courtesy of Hayward Tyler Magazine early 1980s

Introduction by Georgina Cook

*M*y husband, Colin Cook, was a lovely, kind and gentle man. I met him in 1962 when I was 19 and he was 26. We were married for over 41 years until he passed away after a long illness on 1st December 2007. When Colin retired, he had more time to read and research local history. Just before he died, Colin published a book "The Story of Limbury-cum-Biscot", but sadly he didn't live long enough to know how well it sold. He had also written other articles about the local area and his own life. I have gathered together some of his writings and added some facts of my own. His stories follow, but first I will tell you a bit about Colin . . . .

From the Eulogy at Colin's funeral -

"Colin Raphalge Cook was born in Luton on 17th April 1936 and went to school at Tennyson Road & Surrey Street. He had two younger sisters, Pat and Margaret. In his youth he joined the Boys Brigade, working his way up to Captain of 1st Luton Company. He helped to organise reunions of the company in May 2001 and October 2007 but was very disappointed not to be able to attend the latter due to ill health.

Colin's working life began with an apprenticeship at Hayward Tyler & Co, and he worked there for 33 years until being made redundant in 1985. He worked for other pump companies, including KSB, Ingersoll Rand and Wier Pumps, which meant increased travel to London and, for two years, Northfleet near Gravesend, which required his leaving home Monday morning and returning Friday evening. A further year at Hayward Tyler & Co, followed by 18 months at Halfords in Luton and Hitchin, concluded his career and he retired, due to ill health, at the age of 64. He wrote a book about the early days of the Hayward Tyler company, part of which they are hoping to publish for their 200 year anniversary in 2015. One of his last outings was a tour of the factory with the Hayward Tyler Pensioners' Association.

In 1962, Colin met Georgina (Gina) Trustam at the Victor Silvester Dancing School held at the Odeon Cinema in Dunstable Road. They were married at Holy Trinity Church Biscot in 1966 and Colin subsequently joined the Church and in later years was Churchwarden there for 13 years. During this time he became particularly interested in the churchyard, successfully locating many a grave upon request. He also helped at many interments of ashes, becoming well known to local funeral directors. His retirement from this post in 2005 was once again due to failing health.

Colin and Gina had two sons; Peter, born in November 1967, and Derek in May 1970. Colin always made it very clear he was proud of them and their achievements. Peter went to Leicester University and gained his BSc in Astrophysics and then a PhD in Atmospheric Physics at UMIST in Manchester, going on to do scientific research at universities in London, Cambridge, Manchester and Norwich. Derek joined Covenant Players International Christian Drama Group and was sent to Germany, where he met Lotta, a Swedish girl in the same group as he was, and married her two years later. They settled in Sweden and it wasn't too long before Colin became a Grandad. Zoe was born in 1998 and Elliot in 2001. (Melody was born in 2008, three months after Colin passed away.) Colin and Gina made regular visits to Sweden to see their grandchildren, and the family make regular visits to England.

Colin was also a member of "Friends of Luton Museums" and the U3A Historical Society and spent many years collecting "antiques". In 1976 he bought himself a 1936 Austin Seven "Ruby" Saloon and for over twenty years attended many car rallies. He was very sad when he could no longer tinker with the Austin and had to sell it in 2005.

Colin had always been interested in anything to do with industrial and social history and collected so many items over more than 20 years that he had his own "museums" in the back garden. There is a Blacksmith Shop and collections of farm implements, office equipment through the ages from the abacus to the computer, shoemaking tools, plumbing tools, items from an old foundry, "kitchenalia", cameras and magic lanterns etc, sewing machines and many other collections. He enjoyed showing people all his treasures. Many people have been to visit and it has been featured twice on Three Counties Radio.

In later years Colin spent a lot of time writing and giving talks on a variety of subjects to many and varied groups in Luton and Dunstable. For him the past was very much a living thing and researching Social History was a labour of love".

 **Colin Cook** was born in Luton in 1936 and always lived in the town. After his apprenticeship with Hayward Tyler from 1951 to 1956 he worked for the Company in the Sales Office for a further 29 years before being made redundant in 1985. He then worked for other major pump companies in London and Gravesend before returning to Hayward Tyler in 1997 for a further year.

Colin published his first book, "The Story of Limbury-cum-Biscot", at the end of November 2007 but very sadly passed away in December, after a long illness. His wife, Georgina marketed his book and had more printed in the spring of 2008.

Colin also wrote the History of Hayward Tyler & Co and a book about Apprentices through the Ages and, although they were never published, copies of these manuscripts are available for reference in Luton Library.

Colin's hobbies included astronomy, archaeology and antiques and he owned a 1936 Austin 7 Ruby car for nearly 30 years which he regularly drove to rallies. He also had a large collection of old agricultural equipment, kitchenalia and other artefacts covering social and industrial history which he kept in "museums" in the garden. Colin gave many talks about various aspects of his interests.

Georgina has collected together some of Colin's writings about the local area and stories about his life into this book to celebrate his memory.

Contents

Part One

Colin's Museum Collection   1

Part Two

Colin's Writings

Chapter 1 – Growing up in Luton in Wartime   21

Chapter 2 – An Apprentice Remembers   39

Chapter 3 – A Short History of Hayward Tyler   51

Chapter 4 – Into the Fens   71

Chapter 5 – Memories of Ruby   84

Chapter 6 – A Visit to a Hat Factory   95

Chapter 7 – A Walk from Luton to Biscot   103

Chapter 8 – The Crawley Family Legacy   111

Appendix   125

Part One

Colin's "Museum" Collection

C olin always loved old things and started to collect items over thirty years ago. I didn't realise how much he had stored away until we had friends round for tea one day and he got everything out on display on tables under the carport. He had been storing things in the loft and also in the bottom of his wardrobe. The friends were all very impressed and, I must admit, so was I.

Early Days of Collecting

In 1985 Colin was made redundant from Hayward Tyler & Co and he used some of his redundancy money to buy a small shed and install it at the bottom of the garden to house his treasures. Colin didn't specialise in any one area, although, at this stage, it was mainly old kitchen items. Soon he branched out and started to collect anything and everything old, including farming equipment, blacksmith items, office equipment, cameras and magic lanterns, old bottles, smoking equipment, things from the war, one of the first vacuum cleaners (Wizard - 1912) and one of the first washing machines (Darling Washer - 1926), old mangles and other assorted household items. The old vacuum cleaner was spied in an antique shop in Glossop when we were on holiday in the Peak District and it came home on the back seat of our car.

Wizard Vacuum Cleaner 1912

When Burgess Bros Iron Foundry in Albert Road, Luton closed down in 2000, Colin was allowed to go in and collect as many things as he could before everything was taken away. At that time Luton Museum was unable to salvage or store any of the items.

Items from Burgess Bros Iron Foundry in Albert Road, Luton
1883-2000

From 1981 for nearly twenty five years we went to car and steam rallies with the old Austin and Colin found many old bits and pieces for his collection. We always returned with something he had purchased. The Austin was not very big but somehow we always managed to get things home. When our sons were young they came to the rallies with us and would be holding onto, or sitting on, all sorts of things on the way home. (Colin writes about his Austin Seven Ruby car in Chapter 5 of the second part of this book.)

Patterns from Burgess Bros Iron Foundry in Albert Road, Luton
1883-2000

Colin also bought many items from the Auction House, Luton, which was then in John Street and later in Crescent Road. A lot of items just looked like rusty bits of metal to start with, but Colin would clean them up and paint them. Usually they would be painted black for non-moving parts and red for the bits that moved. He would spend many happy hours in the garage with wire brushes and sandpaper removing rust. Friends would also donate their family treasures to Colin; we would often return home to find items on the doorstep. This was very kind of them but I think many thought it a good way to part with things they no longer wanted but couldn't bring themselves to throw away. Colin managed to find room for, and treasured, everything.

On our trips to steam rallies with the Austin car we came across Stan Martin of Martin's Sheds of Bassingbourn near

Royston, Hertfordshire, who often had a stand there displaying his sheds, garden seats, etc. He would eventually make various sheds for us to whatever specifications we gave him. As Colin's collection got bigger we cleared different areas of the garden, put down slabs as a base and contacted Stan for another shed. Soon we had three sheds and a summerhouse built to accommodate different areas of interest.

Whenever Stan came along with his workers to erect a new shed it was a great occasion. The biggest shed we had built was L-shaped and was 18 feet long by six feet deep with the L-shape at one end nine feet deep. Some sections were too big to get under the carport and round through the side gate into the back garden, so Stan got permission from the local school to bring his lorry round onto the school field at the bottom of our garden and lift the sections over the fence. I have a vivid memory of Stan perched on top of the school fence, with his fellow workers trying to help him over and then lifting all the sections over to put them together. Fortunately the sheds always fitted on the bases we had got ready for them.

Stan Martin scaling the school fence to set up the biggest shed

Bringing the shed sections over the school fence

I had been afraid this number of sheds would overpower our medium sized garden but they fitted very neatly around at the end of the garden and give us good protection from the prevailing wind and weather. We also had a breeze block building built onto the back of the garage to house the blacksmith shop.

"Museum" sheds in the garden

Colin's "Museum" Collection

*Part of Blacksmith Collection
with London Anvil (late 19th
century) in Foreground*

*Part of the Blacksmith
Collection*

Forge with Foot Bellows – Early 20th century

7

We modelled the different sections of the museum to look like the exhibits in the museum at Stockwood Park, Luton, and we labelled the different items with information. People began to visit and look around and Colin loved talking to them about his collection. One friend contacted Three Counties Radio and in February 2004 Martin Coote came to interview Colin as they walked round the collection, viewing all the items on display. At the time Colin hadn't realised Martin was actually recording so he was quite shocked when at twenty to one Martin said he had to rush off because he was on the air at one o'clock that day and it would be broadcast then. I arrived home from work at five to one to find Colin in quite a panic trying to find out how to record the programme. Luckily we were able to record it and I have the recording to listen to whenever I like.

About the same time, three young men from Luton University came to interview and video Colin and his collection as part of a project for their degree course on people who were collectors. Colin got the old Austin out of the garage for them to video too and treated them to a tune on his 100 year old phonograph, playing one of his wax cylinders, and this was used for some of the music on the video.

We had a request from the Austin A30 Car Club from Caddington to hold one of their regular meetings in our garden, and one summer evening about 20 members arrived and enjoyed wandering round the garden viewing all the sheds with the various collections. They were also treated to music on the phonograph.

Twice we were invited to make a display of old items at Meppershall Summer Fete and Colin took his Austin and lots of old farming equipment to show people. The first year a small horse box was used to transport the items but by the next year we had a small trailer and I drove our ordinary car towing things over there while Colin drove the Austin. We had a very enjoyable time talking to everyone and telling them about everything.

Colin's "Museum" Collection

Austin A30 Car Club holding their meeting in our garden

Our Stall set up at Meppershall Summer Fete

In November 2009, Justin Dealey from Three Counties Radio did a live broadcast from my garden at 7.30am following an article in the Luton News about me showing visitors Colin's Collection to raise money for the new Church Hall being built at St Thomas's Church in Stopsley. The Vicar, Reverend David Alexander, had given members of the congregation £5 each to use to make more money towards building costs, so I provided tea and biscuits and charged £1 for viewing all the items. I was very lucky that it was always good weather whenever people visited.

Friends from St Thomas's Church on a visit to the "Museums"

There had been an article in the Luton News about Colin soon after he died. Beverley Creagh from the Luton News came to interview me about the book he had written, "The Story of Limbury-cum-Biscot". Colin was a well known local historian and he had given many talks locally. While Bev was with me, she looked at the collection and was so interested that she arranged for it to be videoed and put onto the internet for the Luton News / Herald Newspapers.

It had been hoped that Woodside Animal Farm would be able to set up the collection at their Leisure Centre as a permanent educational attraction for visitors but unfortunately this has not been possible. I hope that one day it will be possible for the collection to be given to the local area and kept together for people to be able to view and appreciate all Colin's hard work. It would be a fitting memorial to Colin. However, should we not be able to save the collection as a whole, there may be collectors who would be interested in acquiring an individual section of the museum to add to their own collection.

Georgina Cook 2012

I am very grateful to Mr Dennis Goodyear from Stockwood Park Discovery Centre for his help and advice on making an inventory of all the objects in Colin's collection.

Many thanks also to Mr John Kairis for his photographs of many of the items.

Office Equipment from the Abacus to the Computer

Magic Lanterns

Mincers, Shredders, Slicers etc.

Kitchen Equipment

Mangles and Washing Items

17 guinea Sewing Machines

Farming Tools

Hand Tools and Shoe Mending Equipment

Cameras

Projectors

Smoking and Shaving Items and Early Mineral Water Bottles

Hand Tools - Roller, Plough and Seeders

Part Two
Colin's Writings
Chapter 1
Growing Up in Luton

My parents were not Lutonians but came from Oare, a village in Kent. In October 1931, my father's parents, my parents, who were engaged at this stage, and my father's younger three brothers and three sisters, moved to Luton. His two elder sisters, both married, decided to remain in Kent. The move from Kent by the whole family was, in the main, for economic reasons; the hungry thirties were well named. My grandfather originally came from the Birmingham area and had considered moving back there, but my grandmother had relations in Luton and, after a holiday there, decided that Luton held better prospects.

Arriving in Luton, the family moved into a large three bedroom terraced house in Harcourt Street, up on the "bank". The front bedroom was occupied by the four girls, the middle bedroom by the four boys, and my grandparents were sleeping in the small bedroom at the back. It must have been very cramped, with little privacy.

My parents were married in the September of 1934 at St Paul's Church in Hibbert Street and went to live at 32, Arthur Street, which must have eased congestion at the family home. I was born there on 17th April 1936. In 1938 my parents and I moved to 35, Tennyson Road. My father's second eldest sister and her family came to live in our old house in Arthur Street.

My early memories are very hazy and I can only assume that my pre-school years followed a non-eventful path with visits to Bulls, the chemist in Castle Street, to be weighed and checked over by Mr Bull every few weeks, and the occasional holiday to Ramsgate and visits to mother's relations in Faversham, Kent.

At the age of about eight years old children reach a stage of collecting and joining. Suddenly they get the urge to collect all kinds of articles and join clubs and activities. It is a marker in the stage of growing up and is just as true now as it was in my childhood days. I started to collect cigarette cards, stamps, coins and matchbox tops, there was a wide variety available. I also collected (now to my shame) birds' eggs, and had a fine collection. Swaps were made at school and in the evenings to improve my collections.

I had always fancied dressing up and singing, so it was no surprise to my parents when I decided to join St Paul's Church Choir. We rehearsed on Thursday evenings and sang twice on Sundays plus the occasional Saturday wedding. It was an all male choir with a dozen or so boys of the soprano range, and we were prone to inattention and whispering. It took the choir mistress all her strictness and forcefulness to keep us under control during choir practice and services. Her whip hand was in not allowing anyone misbehaving to sing at a wedding. This meant missing out on a shilling, a lot of money then for an eight year old.

About this time, together with a few friends, I decided to join the Wolf Cubs at King Street Congregational Church. I also joined the Boys Brigade at Union Street Baptist Church. I couldn't do both so left the Cubs but kept with the Boys Brigade. I made many lifelong friends and spent many happy years there and eventually rose in the ranks to be Captain of the 1st Luton Company.

In 1957 I moved with my family to 104, Harcourt Street,

where I stayed till I was married in 1966 and then moved to Stopsley.

Wartime Luton

Just after the destruction of the twin towers in New York on 11th September 2001, I was asked to speak to sixty 7 to 8 year olds at a local school on this same subject, and told not to frighten the children. I need not have worried. Children are very resilient and they do not dwell on a subject for very long.

They wanted to know, did I fight on the Russian Front? (I was only seven at the time). What was it like outside the house during the war? I countered by showing them fire fighting equipment, stirrup pumps, tin helmets and gas masks. I had taken with me my ventriloquist's dummy 'Charlie' and while the boys got involved with the pumps and helmets, the girls took turns in holding Charlie down on the table and putting a gas mask on his head. I was asked "does Charlie really speak?". I had to confess it was me. At the end I gave each of them 1 week's war ration of sweets - they were not impressed.

Even without the War you would find Britain a much different place to live in; for a start there were no teenagers, you would be considered to be a child until you left school at 14 years and then you were a young adult. You either dressed as a child or as a young man or woman. There was no Pop Music or Pop Groups. Imperial measurements were used for length (feet and inches) and weights (lbs and ozs) and there were 240 pence in every pound.

When the War started all street lights were turned off and black curtains were put up at all the windows in the house so that no light could shine through. This was done so that at night villages and towns could not be seen from the air. If a light was seen coming from a house, an air raid warden would shout "put that light out". Another change was the taking down of all the road sign posts so that any invading enemy would not know where they were. The trouble was we did not know either. We were all given identity cards, so we knew who we were, but not where we were.

As a three year old the outbreak of war on 3rd September 1939 did not worry me over much although, in retrospect, I must have been aware of the change in tempo of every day life. When the war started, children who lived in large cities, which due to expected air raids were the most dangerous places to live, were moved to country locations or towns which were considered to be low risk areas. During the first week following the outbreak of war, evacuees from London, mainly children, arrived at my local school Tennyson Road and the teachers, with helpers, distributed them around the area. A lady knocked on our door and when mother opened it she was confronted by a sea of little faces. Mother was asked if she would take in two children; she was not very enthusiastic but settled on two sisters aged, I suppose, 8 and 6. Our next door neighbours, Mr and Mrs Windmill, were given one boy as they had no children of their own; it must have been agreed that one would be enough. The boy was about my age, an ideal playmate. The arrangement of having evacuees living with you was not easy and friction arose between my mother and the girls' parents and within six months they had returned to London. The women who looked after the evacuees were given 10/6d per week for the first child and 8/6d for the second, to cover food and clothes. Ten shillings in 1939 has a purchasing power of approximately £25 today.

In preparation for war, four tunnels had been constructed in Luton and one, called the Albert Road Tunnel, ran under the road from the Baker Street entrance outside Bailey Street Methodist Church to an entrance halfway down Albert Road, with another entrance at New Town Street. Tunnel marshals were appointed to keep order. Tunnels were also dug in school playgrounds.

My sister, Patricia Ann, was born on 12th July 1940 and soon made her presence felt; this was a shock for me having to share my parents' time with her. Unlike the evacuees she was here to stay. In Castle Street, Mr Bull the chemist weighed the new born babies in his shop. This was done each week to make sure that the children were gaining weight at the correct rate. There was no National Health Service then. Mr Bull made up his own medicines to meet our needs; it was cheaper than visiting the Doctor.

In the summer of 1940 my father put up, with the help of two young lads whose garden backed on to ours, one of Mr Anderson's air raid shelters. Once the hole was dug to accommodate the shelter there was very little garden left, just enough for Mother's washing line and a small strip for flowers. (My Auntie Beat had an inside Morrison shelter which doubled as a dining table.) We did not use the Anderson shelter very much, preferring to sleep downstairs. My sister and my Auntie Win and I slept in the cupboard under the stairs, Auntie and I sleeping on the floor and my sister on a shelf above. My parents slept in the living room beside the door of the cupboard and would join us should the need arise. This cupboard was also used for magic lantern slide shows which took our minds off reality.

On Friday afternoon 30th August that year my parents took my baby sister and me for a walk down to the town to go shopping at the Co-op in New Bedford Road, not one of the best days to venture out. That afternoon 194 bombs fell on Luton. We took shelter in a warehouse across the road from the Co-op and were safe, but 59 people of Luton lost their lives. Hurrying back home after the all clear had sounded, we found all the windows broken and the backdoor leaning against the kitchen dresser. I took fright, going to my friend's house in Harcourt Street which was now a hole in the ground with just the staircase standing. He and his family had sheltered under the stairs and were safe. I ran on to my grandparents' house which was in a similar state to our own but they were all OK. After we had all calmed down we realised how lucky we were, although we did not go shopping so often. Although we had many warnings, only 2 V1 flying bombs (Doodlebugs) fell on Luton; this was in the early hours of 21st June 1944 causing only a few minor injuries. However, like a bolt from the blue, a V2 rocket landed in Biscot Road just before 10.00am on 6th November 1944 between the dispatch department of Commer-Karrier Ltd and a row of houses. The death toll of 19 was the second highest of any Luton incident and 196 people were injured. The government spin doctors, so as not to cause a panic for we had no way of stopping the V2 rocket, said it was a gas explosion. In London there were many such explosions and the people of London started to call them flying gas stoves.

Within the first few months of the war each person was issued with a gas mask as fear from a gas attack was very real. Thank goodness it never happened. The adults had boring standard gasmasks, while the children were given ones with a Mickey Mouse design to encourage them to wear them. They had two large eyes and a rubber floppy nose. For the very young children and babies special respirators were provided, the child was placed inside the canvas container which had a viewing panel and straps tied to make the container as air tight as possible. Fixed to the container was an air pump (bellows type) to provide a flow of air to the child. I recall being shown by my father how to operate the pump should the occasion arise, while my sister, frightened of being enclosed in the container, cried loud and clear. Mother, as I recall, was not amused by our endeavours.

The first major upheaval in my life was when I started school in the summer of 1941 at Tennyson Road Infants and Juniors School. The school from the Harcourt Street entrance (Junior Girls and Infants only) was much higher than the road and was approached by three flights of steps, flanked on either side by foreboding trees and shrubs. At the top were two entrances; one engraved over the door "Girls" and the other "Infants". I was

Child's "Mickey Mouse" gas mask

not keen on going but Mother held me in a vice-like grip and propelled me up the flights of steps and into the school entrance for "Infants". Until then I did not know I was an Infant. I found out afterwards that there were three kinds of children at the school - Junior Boys, Junior Girls and Mixed Infants. I hoped they would put me in the correct category when I reached 7 years old.

On the first day labelling was my least concern. Mother had left me at the classroom and gone home and I wanted to go home too. Hats and coats were taken off the new inmates by the teachers, and we were sat down on forms, two at a desk. We numbered, I suppose, about forty pupils. Having arrived, I had made up my mind not to stay and waited for the classroom door, now firmly closed, to open. My chance came when another teacher came into the room and left the door slightly ajar; I was near the door and in a flash I was in the corridor and making for home. The shouts behind me only spurred me on; I reached the flights of steps and was half way down the second flight when a hand descended upon my shoulder and I was frog-marched back to my classroom. During that first week I made a number of attempts to escape school, at one time reaching my front door before being hauled back there.

After that first week I settled down to being an infant and began to enjoy the lessons. Along the wall behind the teacher's desk were the letters of the alphabet depicting animals and familiar objects. We would sit in front of these on individual coloured elliptical rush mats and recite the alphabet and objects in unison, after which questions were asked. We also recited the times tables up to 5 times ten (6 and above were for juniors); the pence table was also tried. Thus I have always felt that singing through the tables was an excellent way to learn; even the dimmest would know that $4 \times 4 = 16$ and $5 \times 7 = 35$.

The lavatory block (unheated) serving both the infants and the junior girls stood at the far end of the infants' playground. The infant boys were served by two cubicles, enclosed and roofed, and a urinal which took up the end of the block. The urinal accommodated up to eight boys at a time but did not have a roof; it could therefore be very unpleasant in wet and windy weather. Children did not find this at all unusual, as most houses at this time had outside lavatories, and it was then considered unhealthy to have lavatories inside the house.

The infant children divided by gender at playtime. The boys played all kinds of running games from kick-and-run football to Cowboys and Indians. The girls skipped, stood in circles reciting rhymes or stood upside-down, with heads on their coats, against the high wall separating the infants from the junior boys' playgrounds, showing all next week's washing.

Every so often we had a visit from Sister Nora, the Nit

Explorer. We were called into a room about six at a time and made to face the wall, not looking from side to side. Then Sister Nora groomed our hair with a special comb. This was also done at home; I used to sit on a chair with a sheet of paper on my lap while Mother combed my hair to see if any nits jumped out.

It was not until I transferred to the juniors that I experienced air raids at school. We had many gasmask practices in class, the teacher would say "Quickly and quietly three in a form and see how still you can sit with your gasmasks on". (The form and desk formed one piece of furniture designed for two children and we all moved to the left and squashed in). The teacher was then confronted with forty Mickey Mouse faces: for the children's masks were made attractive to encourage the wearing of them. The children carried their gasmasks with them at all times and would be sent home for failing to bring them to school.

Children with their "Mickey Mouse" gas masks

At the sound of the air raid warning each class complete with gas masks would march in twos, not run, in a predetermined order to the underground shelter in the boys' play-ground. When all were in, the large steel doors were closed, and we sat in the dark on long wooden forms; masks were only put on when we were told. At the end of each corridor by the light of a hurricane lamp the teacher would read a story or we sang our times tables and songs. This was much more fun than lessons and we all groaned when the all clear was sounded and the steel doors opened.

When an air raid was on, men and women called wardens used to patrol the streets looking out for fires; they carried with them a stirrup pump and a bucket and wore a steel helmet and blue boiler suit.

During the war there was no television and even before the war very few people had television, as they were very expensive. The television service had only started in Britain in 1936, the range of the broadcast was very limited and there was only one station broadcasting for two and a half hours a night. The service was suspended until after the war; people spent the majority of their free evenings at home and the wireless programmes became very popular for all ages, with programmes such as "Monday Night at Eight O'Clock", "In Town Tonight", "Life with the Lyons" with Ben Lyon, Bebe Daniels, Richard, Barbara and Vic Oliver, "Children's Hour" with Uncle Mac and "Larry the Lamb", and "ITMA" (It's That Man Again). ITMA was so popular it was said that if Hitler had invaded between 8.30 and 9 o'clock on a Thursday night he would not have found anybody about. "Sincerely Yours" presented by Vera Lynn and programmes with Rob Wilton (when war broke out) were great favourites. Today TV programmes such as Dad's Army, Hallo-Hallo and Goodnight Sweetheart, plus films and documentaries, try to bring back those times. Our wireless was powered by battery accumulators which required recharging at the local barber's shop. Children could become Ovaltineys which was a very popular children's programme. I heard on the television recently that Hitler was an Ovaltiney but when he invaded Poland he had to send his badge back.

The songs we used to sing were – "We'll Meet Again" and "The White Cliffs of Dover" with Vera Lynn and "Sing As We Go" with Gracie Fields. Other popular songs were – "Yes we have no bananas", "Roll out the Barrel", "A Nightingale Sang in Berkeley Square" and "I'm going to get lit up when the lights go on in London". George Formby was in great demand, as were the Henry Wood Promenade Concerts.

Popular films were Walt Disney's "Snow White", Noel Coward's "In Which We Serve", "Gone with the Wind" and "Brief Encounter".

When the war started, ice cream and lollies disappeared from the shops. Because at this time very few people had a refrigerator or a freezer, we could not make our own ice cream or lollies. Few people at this time had an electric washing machine, the vacuum cleaner was a novelty and the dishwasher, the computer and videos were still in the future. Without a refrigerator, freezer or washing machine meant that the wife/mother spent a great time of her day doing hard physical housework and shopping every day for fresh food (no supermarkets). I remember Pease Pudding bowls on the windowsills on a Friday night. The coming of the war, food shortages and queues for everything made great demands on women's lives. The result was that the majority of them had neither the time nor energy to hold down a job outside of the home.

The war meant shortages of everything, especially food, and rationing was the only fair way to ensure that everyone had enough to eat. In theory the Government made sure it did not repeat the problems of food distribution of the First World War, for there were always shortages of supply and the Black Market was there for those in the know. I remember Mother buying half a sheep's head from the butchers shop to make brawn for tea.

A week's ration of food per person in 1945 was as follows:
2½ pints of Milk, children had an extra third of a pint per day at school
2oz Tea (1 oz equals 28 grams)
2oz Butter
3oz Soap (shaving soap was not rationed)
1 Egg
4oz Margarine
4oz Jam
8oz Sugar
3oz Cheese
2oz Lard
4oz Biscuits
3oz Bacon
4oz tin of Sardines
16oz Meat
4oz Corned Beef
3oz Chocolate or Sweets - a number of adults and children used to suck cough sweets and Horlicks tablets to eke out the ration and some mistook OXO cubes for chocolate, what a shock for them.

Oranges, lemons, grapefruit and bananas disappeared from the shops. Bread was not rationed until after the war and you could always get potatoes and vegetables at a price, also rabbits and chickens. Fish was also not rationed, however at the fish and chip shop you had to supply your own wrapping paper as paper was in short supply. Sometimes even beer and tobacco ran out of supply and some tried to brew their own beer, and evil smelling substances were put into cigarettes and pipes.

By the time the war started cereals such as Kellogg's Corn Flakes started to appear on the breakfast table, although it took time to change from a cooked meal. Rationing however changed the eating habits of a large section of the population.

Clothes were also put on ration and the slogan of the time

was "Make do and mend" and many became experts at sewing and making clothes from old materials. Stockings were also in very short supply and girls used to stain their legs with tea and draw a black pencil line down the back of their legs to look like a seam. "Waste not Want not" was also a slogan of the time, relating to all kinds of goods but mainly referring to food. A large proportion of goods including foods were imported and our ships had to risk being sunk by German warships.

Toys were also in very short supply and it was a case of either making them yourself or making do with second-hand toys (swapped or bought).

Sunshine must also have been in short supply for I remember going to the hospital once a week and sitting in a room with a number of other children all in "the all together" with just goggles on, playing under very bright and warm lamps.

A few weeks before D Day many side roads near us were used to hold troops and trucks before moving down to the coast. This was a great time for us children, the troops made a great fuss of us giving us sweets and chocolates. It also perked up the lives of many of the young women (so I have been told, I was too young to notice at the time).

The War years were of course a terrible time and for many great suffering, but there were many lighter moments of fun and laughter, which we should not forget. The War brought people together in a very special way.

Wartime Memories

The Wartime covers my pre and early school days, as such memories are only snippets of that time. Where memory had failed me, my mother explained to me the circumstances and details of a particular incident which I vaguely recalled, when preparing a talk at a much later date.

I trust these memories will be of some help to you.

London Evacuation Facts

For London schools, the 2nd World War meant evacuation and the biggest ever disruption of the education system. London had made full evacuation plans before the 1938 Munich crisis and drew upon the experiences gained during the Jubilee in 1935 and the Coronation of 1937. Then large numbers of school children, 70,000 in 1935 and 37,000 in 1937, were assembled. Both these peace-time logistic exercises had shown how large numbers of school children under the control of their own teachers could be moved from all points of the London compass by public transport.

As the outbreak of war became imminent, the plans were brought to a stand-by stage. Before the summer term ended on 19th July 1939, a full scale rehearsal involving 5,000 children and their teachers was carried out in Chelsea, with only minor snags, which helped to show what to avoid when the real thing came.

On 14th August the key staff were recalled from holiday and on 25th August the schools were reassembled and plans tested. The evacuation order was received on Thursday, 31st August to be put into operation the following day. The Education Department was also responsible for the evacuation of old people and pregnant women. At the last minute plans were speeded up by the Ministry of Health, such that the four day programme was telescoped into three which caused minor chaos.

There were 1,589 assembly points, 168 stations from which parties departed and 271 stations where they were set down. Altogether about 287,000 persons left London on the first day and by the morning of the fourth day some 600,000 had been moved out of the Greater London area. This total of 600,000 was made up of 200,000 school children, 160,000 pre-school children, 160,000 mothers with children, 10,000 expectant mothers, 5,000 blind and cripples, 65,000 helpers, physical and mental defectives and hospital patients. Two days before war was declared 5,000 London school children were evacuated to Luton, followed by a number of blind people and expectant mothers. Many were to return home within the year.

Corner Shops around where Colin lived as a boy -
Mrs Bell - Groceries in Tennyson Rd / Harcourt St
Mrs Lines - Green Grocer in Tennyson Rd / Cowper St
Mr & Mrs Shooter - Milk, Dairy Products and Eggs in Tennyson Rd / Cowper St
Mr & Mrs Desbrough - Bakers in Tennyson Rd / Cowper St
Mr Osbourne - Butcher in Tennyson Rd / Baker St
Mr Howlet - Groceries in Harcourt St / Ashton Rd
Mr Bert Laurence - Green Grocer in Cowper St / Ashton Rd
Mr Tompkins - Paper Shop in Cowper St / Ashton Rd
Mr Coe - Hair Dresser & Accumulator Charging in Ashton Rd
Mrs Coe - Stationery and Knitting Equipment etc in Ashton Rd / Arthur St
Fish and Chip Shop in Ashton Rd
Cobblers Shop in Ashton Road
Mr Leslie Laurence - Coal Merchant with Horse, also in Cowper St

Comparing Money in World War II with Purchasing Power in 2000

Money during World War II	Written as	Common Name	Purchasing Power in 2000
Farthing	¼d	Farthing	£0.05
Halfpenny	½d	Ha'penny	£0.10
Penny	1d	Penny	£0.21
Three Pence	3d	Thrup'nny bit	£0.62
Sixpence	6d	Tanner	£1.24
Shilling	1s or 1/-	Bob	£2.49
Florin	2s or 2/-	Two Bob Bit	£4.97
Half Crown	2s 6d or 2/6	Half a Crown	£6.22
Ten Shilling Note	10s or 10/-	Ten Bob Note	£24.88
Pound Note	£1 or 20/-	Pound	£49.75

The Home Guard

In early 1940 the Minister for War, Anthony Eden, announced the formation of a Home Defence Force, and called for volunteers. Within 20 hours 250,000 men had visited their local police station to sign up, and within twelve months that figure had risen to a million and a half. The name for this force was to be the Local Defence Volunteers or, as some wag called it Look, Duck and Vanish. At the start this force had no weapons and, until uniforms could be provided, had to make do with a forage cap and an LDV armband. Some members had shotguns and the rest made do with pitchforks and broom handles. When weapons eventually arrived they were rifles of American manufacture and Thompson Sub-machine guns or Tommy Guns, much favoured by gangsters. The LDV soon became known as the Home Guard. In the early days of broom handles and arm-bands they had to put up with a lot of stick from small boys and comedians.

Rob Wilton

The day War broke out my wife said to me "What are you going to do about it?"

I said "I'm going to join the Home Guard"

She said "What will you do?"

I said "Stop Hitler from landing in England"

She said "What, just you?"

I said "No, There will be Harry Evans, Sid Jones and about six others"

She said "Do you know this bloke Hitler?"

I said "Of course not"

She said "How will you know it's him?"

I said "Well, I've got a tongue in my head"

Saturday Morning Pictures (Songs)

Odeon

We come along on Saturday morning, greeting everybody with
a smile,
we come along on Saturday morning knowing it's well worth
while,
As members of the Odeon club we all intend to be,
good citizens when we grow up and fighters of the free.
We come along on Saturday morning, greeting everybody with a
smile, smile, smile, greeting everybody with a smile.

ABC

We are the boys and girls well known as Minors of the ABC
and every Saturday we all line up
to see the films we like and shout aloud with glee.
We have a laugh and have our sing song,
just a happy crowd are we'e.
We're all good pals together, we're Minors of the (shout) ABC.

War Time Songs

It's the Girl that makes the thing
That drills the hole that holds the spring
That works the thing-u-me-bob
That makes the engine roar,

It's the Girl that makes the thing
That holds the oil that oils the ring
That works the thing-u-me-bob
That's going to win the War.

We are the Ovaltineys
Sung by Elsie, Winnie and Johnnie

We are the Ovaltineys, little girls and boys,
Make your requests, we'll not refuse you,
We are here just to amuse you.
Would you like a song or story,
Will you share our joys?
At games or sports we're more than keen,
No merrier children could be seen,
Because we all drink Ovaltine,
We're happy girls and boys.

Colin Cook 2005

Chapter 2

An Apprentice Remembers

(The Author's own recollections)

*T*he Secondary Modern Schools gave a basic all-round education for the 80% of children who failed the "Eleven Plus". The grounding was sound but the science lessons, which incorporated biology, physics and chemistry, consisted of one period a week plus one afternoon for woodwork, hand tools only. This and one period a week for book binding was the extent of our Science & Technology. The Council Careers Officer was surprised that I wished to take up engineering as a career and not the painting and decorating that he had in mind for me.

Like some of the other boys, I applied to a number of engineering companies in the town, sitting entrance examinations and attending interviews. Our knowledge of technical matters in general and engineering in particular was woefully small. However, the school had taught us well in common sense and this, with a few educated guesses, resulted in a good number of us being offered a position in an engineering company. The Personnel Manager at Hayward Tyler, a Mr Stanley Impey, conducted my final interview, a man who, I later realised, was sympathetic and gentle with nervous fifteen year olds.

There were six of us who started work at Hayward Tyler in the early Autumn of 1951. We presented ourselves at 8.30am

HAYWARD-TYLER
& CO LTD · LUTON · BEDFORDSHIRE

LONDON OFFICE:
20, GROSVENOR PLACE
WESTMINSTER, S.W.I
TELEPHONE: SLOANE 7552
T E L E G R A M S
TYLEROX, KNIGHTS, LONDON

PLEASE REPLY TO LUTON

TELEPHONE:
LUTON 395I (FIVE LINES)
T E L E G R A M S:
TYLEROX, LUTON

SHI/JP   2nd July, 1951.

Mr. C.R. Cook,
35 Tennyson Road,
Luton.

Dear Sir,

      As a result of our Selection Tests, we are pleased to offer you a probationary apprenticeship. It will be necessary for you to attend these Works for a medical examination at 12 p.m. on Wednesday the 15th August, when further details will be given you, regarding date of starting, National Insurance Card, and etc.

      There is an Overall Scheme in operation which will be explained to you at this examination for your consideration, if you wish to make use of it.

      Yours faithfully,

      per HAYWARD-TYLER & CO. LTD.

      S. H. Impey
      Personnel Manager.

Colin's offer of a probationary apprenticeship at
Hayward Tyler & Co

to the Personnel Manager's office and, after a formal welcome by the manager, we were taken through what I was to learn was the Heavy Machine and Fitting Shop to the Apprentice Training Centre. Even then I knew I had made the correct choice - the noise, the smells, the vibrations and intensity. I was a little frightened but greatly excited.

Mr Peter Bullock, the Training Officer, was a man with a ready smile but, as we were to learn, he used a firm discipline and he expected us to toe the line, as had our teachers we had just left at school. Mr Bullock, together with his assistant, Mr Jimmy Gilman, introduced us to the vice and file, the two basic elements to master in becoming an engineer.

We were, of course, given overalls to wear. These were rented out to us and cleaned each week by a local laundry, for which a sum was taken from our wages. The starting rate for an apprentice was £2-1-10¾d per week, take-home pay £1-10-0d, of which 15 shillings was given to my mother as a token for board and lodgings.

We felt very conspicuous in our new overalls, especially the first day walking through the factory to the canteen for our midday meal. It was a new experience being in the company of so many adults. As you may well imagine, we came in for many a joke and leg pulling which, because of our tender age, we did not always fully understand. The hours in the training school were 8.30am to 5.30pm (office hours).

The first few months of our training took place at the bench, with files, hacksaws and use of a vertical power drill to hone our skills in exercise pieces and making of tools in steel which we would use in our apprenticeship.

After this time we were introduced to the machines in the Training School namely -

Two Churchill-Redman Cub 6inch Lathes

One Ward 2A Capstan Lathe

One Archdale Vertical Milling Machine

One Milford Tool Grinder

On Wednesdays we attended the local College for Further Education in Park Street, Luton from 9.00am until 7.00pm.

When I was able, I used to walk down to the Blacksmith's Shop, the blacksmith Sid Allen was a surprisingly slight man, but strong. He had two hammer men (strikers) working for him. Sid would indicate with a small two pound hammer where on the hot iron he wished the hammer men to strike. He would strike first and the hammer men followed in a rehearsed order. To stop, Sid would give a double blow with his hammer.

I had spent almost a year in the Training School before my

physique had developed sufficiently for me to enter the Works. My working hours would now be 8.00am to 6.00pm; on Monday and Friday the finishing time was 5.30pm. Saturday morning was part of the normal week but was paid at time and a half.

THE FITTING SHOP

I commenced my apprenticeship training in the Process Pump Fitting Shop (nicknamed the Black Cat Shop due to the poor natural lighting). The Process Pump Shop, like those of other products, was complete in itself, having its own machines, fitters and store keepers committed only to that product. One foreman, with an assistant, oversaw the whole operation. His name was Ernie Abraham, a man who saw apprentices as a necessary evil. I was placed under the wing of a fitter named Arthur Field who viewed me with some apprehension, wondering if piecework rates would be enhanced or not by this small but willing helper. Our relationship lasted just one year. When all was well he called me Charlie but when all was grief I inherited the name John - the percentage was 50/50.

Compared with the other products, the process pumps were considered light weight fitting, even so, the individual item weights could reach 1½cwts and a complete pump and driver from 1½ up to 20cwts. It was at this time that I was introduced to Horace Underwood, a centre lathe turner. A small steel splinter had entered my eye and Arthur sent me to him. Horace was just finishing a cut on his lathe and waved me to his chair. When ready he wiped his hands on a cloth from his pocket, took a magnifying glass and a small rule from his cabinet, adjusted his lamp and tilted back my head. After a brief examination he asked me to relax and look down, rolled back my eye lid with his rule and with a moist piece of cotton wool removed the splinter. I did not feel a thing, he should have been a surgeon. As I went round the works I came across a number of men who had this and other gifts.

THE MACHINE SHOP

I was then transferred to the Submersible Meter/Pump Machine Shop and, under the ever watchful eye of the chargehand, Alec Godfrey, I was introduced to and eventually operated the machines under his control, namely centre lathes, milling machines, slotting and broaching machines and a small surface grinder with which I had an affinity. Alec was a remarkable machinist, able to cut a thread completely by hand and eye, finishing off using a thread chaser.

Colin demonstrating a Centre Lathe Machine in the Training School

THE INSPECTION DEPARTMENT

After completing a year in the Machine Shop, I was transferred to the Inspection Department under the watchful eye of a Mr John Bailey, Chief Inspector. After an initial training period of a few weeks, I was given the responsibility for quality in the same Machine Shop I had just left. I had sets of gauges for bores, threads, etc and my own individual punch to indicate on castings my seal of approval. As you can imagine I felt proud and scared in equal portions. The men in the Machine Shop were on piecework (paid by results) and therefore displeased if I (a mere apprentice) rejected their work. The foreman of the Machine Shop also became upset should his production figures fail by my vigilance to standards. Many an argument took place, but I was supported 100% by Mr Bailey. I often saw him paint the letters "N B G" on certain of the large castings and I later learned this stood for "no bloody good". This surprised me as he never swore, being a Churchwarden and all.

Towards the end of my time in the Inspection Department I was transferred to the Nuclear Clean Fitting Shop. Everything there was as spotlessly clean as a hospital operating theatre. All the fitters wore special hats and shoes, masks and cotton gloves. First thing each morning we had to go round with a duster and vacuum cleaner and then lay out the necessary tools on white paper sheets. After testing, each pump was thoroughly cleaned using solvents and dried using hair dryers before being vacuum packed for despatch. All this high tech work without a computer in sight.

THE DRAWING OFFICE

The next department to benefit from my increasing skills was the Drawing Office. This was the first time I had the experience of working as a member of the staff. The foremost advantage was starting at 8.30am and finishing at 5.30pm instead of 6.00pm. I reported on my first day (in sports jacket and flannels as advised by the Training Officer) to Mr Jack Bryson, Chief Draughtsman. He was a severe disciplinarian who smiled once a day, early in the morning to get it over with. I was assigned to one of the draughtsmen named Cliff Cole who took me under his wing, explaining with great pains elevations, first and third angle projections, printing, layout, etc. He also emphasised that Mr

Bryson did not tolerate general conversation in the office and I was only expected to speak to him if necessary in low tones. This for me was a hard burden to bear. However, Mr Bryson and his wife, who on her own was responsible for printing, left the office each day at noon for an hour's lunch break. This for all the office was Happy Hour, talking broke out everywhere and rubber missiles were not uncommon. As mentioned, Mr Bryson's wife Madge produced prints of our drawings; this took place in the dark room by means of a very large camera mounted on rails. After developing, the drawings were hung on lines by little pegs to dry. Drawings and prints could be collected at 4.00pm and not before, providing drawings were received by 10.00am. I often suspected that she had a sense of humour which her husband kept under tight control.

Also in the office sat three ex-foremen, writing out the spares orders received by the company into large leather-bound books. After about six months my spirit broke out and I was seen by Mr. Bryson in conversation with another draughtsman about the fortunes of Luton Football Club. I was summoned by the word **COOK** to the bottom of the steps leading to his office. I apologised, stating it would not happen again. He agreed it would not happen again and arranged with the Training Officer for me to be removed that week. The next Monday I started work in the Test Bay Office.

THE TEST BAY

My first impression of the Test Bay was that of a large ship's engine room and the Test Bay office, mounted as it was on steel girders 25 feet above the ground, the ship's bridge. The office had large windows on three sides giving an unrestricted view of the Test Bay below which, at first sight, appeared to be a jumble of pipes and bends of all shapes and sizes (up to three feet in diameter), some transporting water, others steam, with cables overhead and gratings covering large water filled pits; some over 20ft deep and 8ft square. Gauges sprouted everywhere like mechanical flowers and the floor was awash with water. Many types and sizes of valves were used, Globe valves for delicate control, Gate valves for quick opening, Non Return valves to ensure the correct direction of flows, and Safety Relief valves. Mr Bill Chambers, the Chief Test Engineer, told me to walk everywhere carefully and slowly.

Second in command was Mr Humphries, who always wore a felt trilby hat to protect his bald head (no hard hats in those days). Watching the various pumps being tested put me in mind of what a ship's engine room must look like. In fact many apprentices when completing their apprenticeship joined the Navy. The pumps and drivers being tested came in all shapes and sizes, some weighing no more than a few cwts others many tons. Large pumps, because of their weight and size, were built on the Test Bay. The largest pump I remember was a vertical reciprocating, compound, duplex, steam pump. It stood 18 feet high, 10 feet wide, and 8 feet in depth. Reciprocating pump tests I found the most dramatic, especially in winter late in the day. Soft lights in the high roof and the flashing of hand held inspection lamps gave the right atmosphere. Before the test started, a small bleed of steam was allowed to enter the steam chest, this was to minimise any thermal shock, and lubricate soft packings. The steam flow was slowly increased until the pump rods started to move, the pump was coming to life and ready for test. All pumps, turbines and motors were given at least an hour's running test, although some would last for days. When the pumps were ready for test with water and steam pipes or electrical cables connected, Mr Chambers would position a test engineer or an apprentice by each valve and gauge as carefully as a cricket captain sets his field. When all was ready and each man at his station, the Customer or Insurance Inspector would emerge from the Test Bay Office walk down the steps to greet Mr Chambers and the test would begin. All eyes were on Mr

Chambers; at his signal a gauge reading was called or a valve wheel turned quickly or given a tweak. An apprentice with Mr Chambers would, on direction, enter figures on a form after Mr Chambers had done the magic with his slide-rule. After the test the Customer Inspector and Mr Chambers would exchange nods and shakes of the head and utter a few grunts. The results on the form were taken to the office where we apprentices would prepare the performance curves and charts. I spent a most enjoyable six months there which ended all too soon.

THE PLANT MAINTENANCE DEPARTMENT

After leaving the Test Bay I spent the remaining six months of my apprenticeship in the Plant Maintenance Drawing Office. This was a small office, sited beside the Plant Foreman's office, consisting of two drawing boards and desks, one for Alan Skeet, the permanent draughtsman, and the other for me. The work was very broad and I soon became Jack of All Trades, assisting Alan and the millwrights in the design of small wall cranes, layout of machine plinths and minor alterations to buildings. The checking of water pipes and sewer gullies were also part of my work. We were involved too in the layout of a test loop for the Nuclear Circulating Pumps and the conversion of the Foundry to a Fitting Shop for the Glandless Motor/Pumps. My foreman in this department was a Mr Bernard Groom, a fair man who left us to our own devices providing the work was completed on time. Again this proved to be a department in which I could willingly launch my career but unfortunately there was not a full time position.

Mr Bullock, the Training Officer, asked me what other department I would like to consider; I said Inspection. The next Monday found me starting work in the Company Sales Department, learning the commercial as well as the technical side of the Company's business. Writing letters to customers with the help of an attractive shorthand typist, the Inspection

Department became a distant memory.

Colin Cook 2003

	Departments in which training was received
DATED 24th April 1952 .	Training Centre Inspection
	Fitting Shop Drawing Office
	Machine Shop Plant Maintenance Offic
	Test Bay

HAYWARD TYLER & COMPANY LIMITED

AND

Charles William Cook

Colin Raphalge Cook

I HEREBY CERTIFY that the within-named

COLIN RAPHALGE COOK

has well and faithfully served the full period of his Apprenticeship in accordance with the terms of the within Deed.

Deed of Apprenticeship

Dated this 15th day of MAY 19 57 .

HAYWARD-TYLER & CO. LIMITED.

the within-named Employer. DIRECTOR.

BLUNDELL, BAKER & CO.,
32 Bedford Row,
London W.C.1.

S.L.S.S.—BS14650-44030

Colin's Deed of Apprenticeship

C. R. COOK

DETAILS OF INDUSTRIAL EXPERIENCE DURING APPRENTICESHIP AND AFTER

First Year in Training School

FITTING :

Details : Filing, Grinding and Drilling using calipers,
micrometer, etc.

MACHINING :

Details : Churchill Centre Lathe. 3 & 4 Jaw Chuck Work,
Between Centres, Screw Cutting, Archdale Vertical Mill.

General work including Gear Cutting using Durding
Head, Centres and Mandrel.

SECOND YEAR FITTING

Details : Filing, scraping, key fitting,
Hand tools, chisels, etc.
Power Tools, Hand Drill, Nut and Stud Runner,
Rotary Grinders.

Preparing castings for pressure tight jointing
and hydraulic testing and striping after test.

Fitting up and assemble centrifugal pumps including
checking alignment.

THIRD YEAR MACHINING.

Details : Snow Surface Grinder, Revolving table.
Edgwick slotting machine
La Point Broaching machine
Long Centre Lathe
Super Finisher
Horizontal Milling Machine

Setting up and operating all machines on general work.

NINE MONTHS INSPECTION

Details : Checking of components (single and batch)
using micrometer, vernier, slip gauges and
hardness tester, etc. Checking assembles and
goods coming into the factory.

Above work on Centrifugal Pumps and Wet Electric
Motors.

ONE YEAR MAIN DRAWING OFFICE

Details : Detail and arrangement also contract drawing of
centrifugal pumps and steam turbines.

Continued

49

-2-

THREE MONTHS TEST BAY

     Details : Preparing test curves and sheets for
                centrifugal pumps.

NINE MONTHS PLANT MAINTENANCE OFFICE

     Details : Detail and arrangement drawings of old and
                new plant including calculations for cranes,
                etc. Also arrangement drawings of buildings.

AFTER APPRENTICESHIP

     Two years Sales Office.

     Details : technical Sales Estimator and Contract Engineer
                for Centrifugal oil process and chemical pumps
                and steam turbines which includes preparation of
                tenders, investigation of projects and advising
                on sub-orders.

For and on behalf of
HAYWARD TYLER & CO. LTD.

Secretary.
23.9.59.

Details of Colin's work experience during his apprenticeship

Chapter 3

A Short History of Hayward Tyler & Co

*P**umps, Automobiles and Water Closets***
This is the story of the firm of Hayward Tyler & Co Ltd, a London Engineering Company who built a factory at Luton in 1872 on a 3½ acre site which was the old cricket ground to the south of Crawley Green Road between the Midland and the Great Northern Railway Lines.

To start the story of Hayward Tyler we must go back to Joseph Bramah, the most versatile of 18th Century engineers. Three portraits hang on the walls of the president's room at the Institution of Mechanical Engineers. From the ends of the room James Watt and George Stephenson face one another. Between them above the president's chair hangs the portrait of Joseph Bramah. During his working life Bramah took out eighteen patents for such inventions as water closets, locks, beer pumps, fire engines and pumps, fountain pens, printing machines, hydraulic presses, carriage brakes and suspension springs, and reciprocating and rotary pumps.

Joseph Bramah was born on 2nd April 1749 in the hamlet of Stainbrough near Barnsley. He was going to spend his life on his father's farm but, due to a leg injury, he was apprenticed to the village carpenter. After completing his apprenticeship he walked the 170 miles to London to seek his fortune. (His leg must have recovered.)

Working in London's great houses as a cabinet maker, he came across the new-fangled water closet. His fertile mind soon came up with modifications, a non-freezing valve and a spiral flush which he patented in 1778. He opened a small workshop and by 1797 had made 6,000 closets; a weekly output of 6.

The Bramah water-closet, his first invention

It is much to the young inventor's credit that, having started with nothing, and with journeymen's wages only about £1 per week, he had saved in the five years he had been working in London the sum necessary to take out a patent, then of the order of £120—nearly half his income.

Joseph Bramah's first invention – his Water Closet

Bramah also became interested in the manufacture of Mineral Waters. Mr William Hamilton in Dublin had produced mineral waters by saturating water with carbonic acid under pressure. Bramah improved on Hamilton's apparatus by using his hydraulic pump and other features, which led him to develop a plant producing 300 bottles of mineral water a day.

HAYWARD-TYLER & CO. LTD.

Single "Bramah" Aerated Water Machine

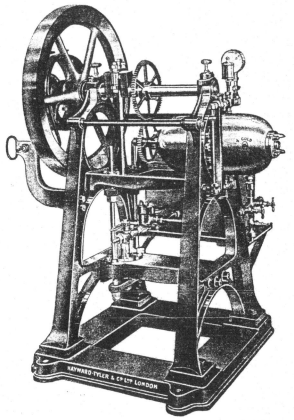

These Machines are for the smaller factories, but turn out just as good quality waters as the larger ones.

Number	Size of Solid Gun-metal Plunger Pump	Contents of Gun-metal Condenser Approx.	Price Complete with Gasometer and Generator	Packing for Shipment	Telegraphic Code	Price of Soda Water Machines only	Packing for Shipment	Telegraphic Code	Fast and Loose Pulleys for Power Code—YITWE
4	1⅜″×4	1¼ Galls.	£112 10 0	£5 10 0	YAACS	£81 0 0	£4 0 0	YAPOK	£5 0 0
1	2 ×5	4 ,,	155 0 0	8 10 0	YAALC	115 0 0	6 12 6	YAREK	5 0 0
01	2½×5	4 ,,	190 0 0	9 10 0	YAAMD	127 12 0	6 12 6	YARIL	included

Glass Saturators attached to any of above .. £9 11 0 extra. Code Word—YITZO

OUTPUT :—1⅜″×4″ Pump—   2″×5″ Pump—   2½″×5″ Pump—
    Soda Water, 15 doz.   Soda Water, 45 doz.   Soda Water, 60 doz.
    Sweet Drinks, 25 doz.   Sweet Drinks, 75 doz.   Sweet Drinks, 95 doz.
    Syphons, 3 doz.   Syphons, 6 doz.   Syphons, 8 doz.

NOTE.—These Outputs are quantities per hour for filling 10-oz. Bottles and 30-oz. Syphons at the following pressure : Sodas, 100 lb. ; Sweets, 60 lb. ; Syphons, 150 lb.

Shipping Measurements.	No. 01 and No. 1.—Machines.	cwt. qr. lb.		No. 4.—Machine.	cwt. qr. lb.
No. 1—Case containing Machine	4′ 0″×3′ 1″×4′ 5″	8 0 0	No. 1—Case containing Machine	3′ 7″×2′ 7″×3′ 6″	5 1 0
,, 2— ,, ,, Generator	2′ 0″×1′ 9″×2′ 0″	3 2 10	,, 2— ,, ,, Generator	1′ 11″×1′ 8″×3′ 6″	2 0 4
,, 3—Gasometer in Tub	4′ 0″×2′ 10″×2′ 10″	1 3 15	,, 3—Gasometer in Tub	3′ 11″×2′ 3″×2′ 3″	1 1 0
,, 4—Wheel	4′ 0″×1′ 0″×0′ 6″	2 2 8	,, 4—Wheel	3′ 0″×3′ 0″×0″ 3′	0 3 14

Bramah Aerated Water Machine

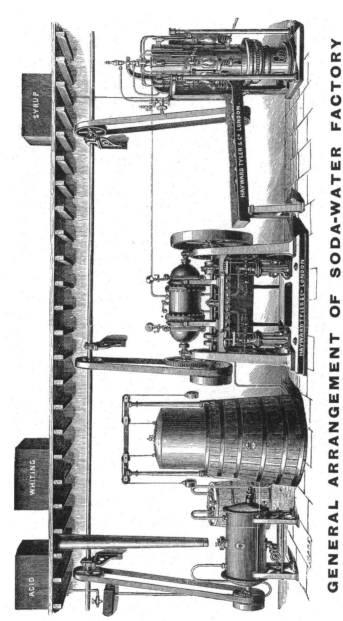

Arrangement of a Soda Water Factory

Joseph Bramah died in 1814 but the company continued trading under the title Bramah and Sons and today is known as Bramah Locks Ltd. Mr William Russell, who was a pupil/employee of Bramah, formed his own company in 1815 manufacturing all the products invented by Bramah except for the locks. Russell died in 1835 and a Mr Hayward Tyler purchased the company from his widow. The Hayward family were Tea Urn manufacturers but Hayward wanted a more exciting life. In 1840 Hayward Tyler took out a patent developing the Soda Water process. From 1835 to 1855 the company continued to prosper but no new products were added. When Hayward Tyler died on 14th September 1855, his widow sold the company to a relative, Mr Robert Luke Howard, for £7,500. So the company passed to the Howard family, who were to remain sole owners until 1957 when they joined the Stone Platt Group.

Water companies were becoming concerned at the amount of water used by the new water closets and encouraged the fitting of water cisterns to control water usage. Having flow control valves in the cistern enabled manufacturers to make the closet basin from ceramics, resulting in beautiful patterns and shapes with mahogany seats, but with pine for the lower classes. To enjoy such luxury today I suggest that you ask to see the toilet and water closet in the house the next time you visit Toddington Manor. In the beginning house owners had trouble with careless servants who were apt to put all kinds of things into the closet basin, so inspection doors were fitted at the "S" bend. Hayward Tyler & Co's interest in this direction included urinals of various shapes, including the popular Bedford with a formed lip, and the Cradle Shell design. Cast iron baths also formed part of the range, including a noiseless hospital bath on rubber wheels with a drag handle – enabling patients to visit other wards while bathing!! This side of the company's business closed in 1935.

The company produced over the years a number of machines for the manufacture and bottling of aerated mineral waters, which

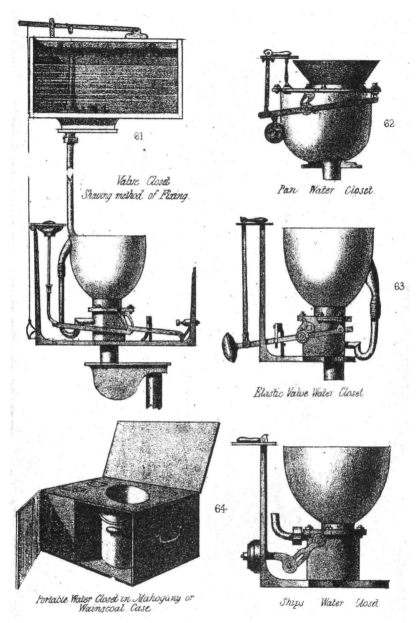

61

Valve Closet
Shewing method of Fixing.

Pan Water Closet.
62

63

Elastic Valve Water Closet.

64

Portable Water Closet in Mahogany or
Wainscoat Case.

Ships Water Closet.

A range of Water Closets produced by Hayward Tyler & Co

304. CAST-IRON BATHS
Without fittings, for Schools, Public Baths, &c.

20½" DEEP INSIDE—PARALLEL SIDES

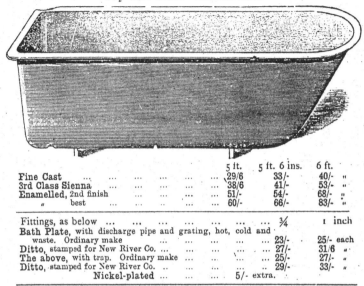

					5 ft.	5 ft. 6 ins.	6 ft.	
Fine Cast	...	...	...	...	29/6	33/-	40/-	"
3rd Class Sienna	...	...	...	...	38/6	41/-	53/-	"
Enamelled, 2nd finish	...	...	...	51/-	54/-	68/-	"
" best	...	...	...	...	60/-	66/-	83/-	"

		¾	1 inch
Fittings, as below			
Bath Plate, with discharge pipe and grating, hot, cold and waste. Ordinary make		23/-	25/- each
Ditto, stamped for New River Co.		27/-	31/6 "
The above, with trap. Ordinary make		25/-	27/- "
Ditto, stamped for New River Co.		29/-	33/- "
Nickel-plated ... ... 5/- extra.			

HAYWARD TYLER & CO.'S

NOISELESS HOSPITAL BATH
OF JAPANNED GALVANIZED IRON

ON WHEELS, WITH RUBBER TIRES, DRAG HANDLE. &c.

304 b.

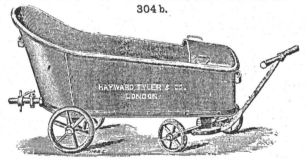

Price, with Draw-off Cock and Union, or Washer and Plug and Union, for convenience of emptying £8 15 0

THIS BATH MAY ALSO BE MADE IN COPPER.

For Bath Valves and Fittings. see pages 62-72, &c.

Delivery: London or Luton. Packing extra.

Weights, &c., approximate. Illustrations not binding as to detail..

1892—ALL FORMER LISTS CANCELLED. SUBJECT TO ALTERATION WITHOUT NOTICE.

Hayward Tyler & Co - Baths

continued up to the 1870s and a new product was introduced in 1863 for making aerated bread in a travelling oven, the first sign of mass production in the food industry. This product was made under licence from a Dr Dauglish.

The business continued to flourish but there was no scope for expansion at the company works in Whitecross Street, London, so the Howards looked further afield and in 1872 secured the present site in Luton.

Straw Hat manufacture was then the major trade in Luton but it gave little occupation for men. It was thought by the directors of the company that it would be easy to obtain labour in Luton. However, it was found that the men were paid by the women to live with them.

The Howards were strong church people and a chapel was set up at the works, services being held before work in the morning. Even up to 1970 services were held on Wednesday afternoons in the club house after closing time.

In 1878 the Rider Hot Air Engine was introduced into the manufacturing range and proved to be a very popular, if cumbersome, source of power. From a leaflet of the time it would seem that it was stoked like an ordinary house or greenhouse stove, readily understood by your gardeners or indoor servants. However, internal combustion engines and the advent of electric motors at the turn of the century saw its demise.

In the 1880s Hayward Tyler & Co took up the system of electric lighting and pioneered conduit wiring. Projects included Holborn Viaduct and Embankment including the dolphin lights. Contracts included churches, hotels, asylums, banks, theatres, offices and ships. At one time Hayward Tyler & Co employed over 50 men in this work alone. However, competition was very strong and after a few years the company returned to its core interests.

In 1890 there were 3 important developments, the first being the employment of a lady secretary by the company - Miss

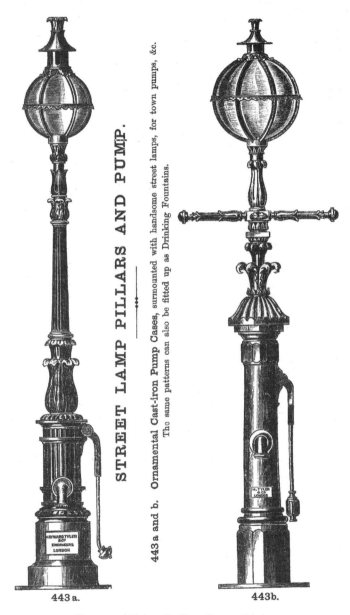

STREET LAMP PILLARS AND PUMP.

443 a. and b. Ornamental Cast-iron Pump Cases, surmounted with handsome street lamps, for town pumps, &c. The same patterns can also be fitted up as Drinking Fountains.

443 a.

443b.

Hayward Tyler & Co - Street Lights

Baylis. Having a female on the books required the engagement of a companion. The next development was that Hayward Tyler & Co introduced a state of the art typewriter (they were one of Remington's first customers), and the third was installing a private telephone extension line to Luton from the London Head office which required an Act of Parliament.

The formation of the Luton Industrial Co-operative Society by the workers of Hayward Tyler was triggered by a works outing in 1882. On the way back from Bedford they had stopped at Silsoe to rest the horses, and the workers, taking the opportunity to stretch their legs, saw a Co-op shop in a side road and felt that Luton should have one too. Obtaining permission from the directors, they held a meeting in the works canteen and from this meeting the Luton Co-operative Society was formed.

At the start of the new century a number of engineering firms became interested in the manufacture of the Motor Car, and in 1903 Hayward Tyler & Co produced the first automobile in Luton. It had a 4 speeds belt drive and the engine developed 6 horsepower at normal running. The car trials were nearing completion when it was consumed in a fire at the works.

Luton Fire Brigade had moved to new premises in 1902 at Amen Corner at the junction of Holly Walk and Church Street. Luton had the advantage of two water towers built on high ground on either side of the Lea Valley and therefore it was unnecessary to have steam operated pumps on the fire tenders. Up to 1914 the Brigade was made up of volunteers. In the early 1900s fire practices were held monthly on a Wednesday evening. On Wednesday, 23rd October 1903 a fire was discovered in the Fitting Shop of Hayward Tyler & Co. Tom Bray, who was just leaving work, ran all the way to the fire station to raise the alarm. It was fortunate that the whole brigade was there, only just finishing their drill and starting their tea of bread and cheese. The bell was rung and the horse was made ready. Within minutes they were setting off at a brisk pace for the works, the officers

Fifteen Reasons why a Motor Car is better than a Horse drawn Vehicle

1. It wants no stable – the coach-house is enough
2. It needs no daily grooming, consequently . . . .
3. No man need be kept specially to look after it
4. There is no manure heap to poison the air
5. It cannot shy, kick or run away
6. It has no will of its own to thwart the wishes of its driver and cause disaster
7. It is more absolutely under control than any horse
8. It costs nothing to keep and cannot "eat its head off in the stable"
9. It consumes only when working, and then in exact proportion to the work done
10. It cannot fall sick and die
11. It will do more work that any two horses and will travel as fast as any one
12. It is only a fraction of the cost in working
13. It can be stopped with certainty and safety in half the distance
14. No cruelty is inflicted by climbing a steep hill with a full load
15. Nor can distress be caused by high speed travelling

Reproduced from Harry Lawson's promotional literature circa 1898

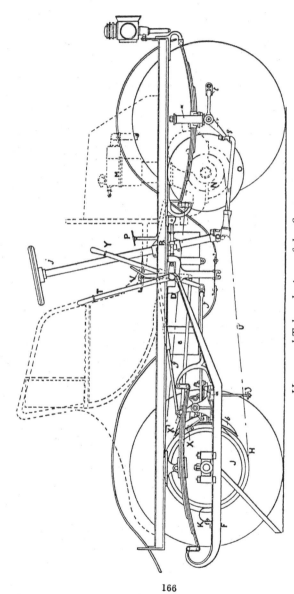

DRAWING OF THE BELT DRIVEN 6 H.P. CAR DESIGNED BY WILLIAM WARBY BEAUMONT AND BUILT BY HAYWARD TYLER LIMITED. THE CAR WAS DESTROYED IN A FIRE AT THE LUTON WORKS ON 23RD OCTOBER 1903 SOON AFTER THE FIRST TESTS OF THE CAR HAD BEEN MADE.

Hayward Tyler design of the first car

166

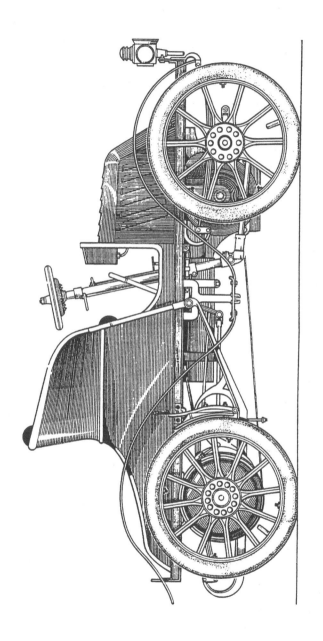

The first car to be manufactured in Luton

seated on the engine and the firemen running behind. When they arrived, the Hayward Tyler workmen tried to help but only succeeded in putting two hoses out of action. Captain Teal, the fire chief, suggested they tackle the fire from the other end of the works. That night Robert Pughe was working late at the London Works when the phone rang to tell him the Luton Works was alight and asked him to inform the directors. As they were not connected to the phone this proved difficult, however, by contacting the nearest police stations, policemen were able to pass on the news. After the fire the rebuilding concentrated not only on the fire damaged works but on extending the house to incorporate the Drawing, Sales and Accounts Offices.

In 1904 the Whitecross Street Works was closed after a period of 64 years and the Sanitary and Mineral Departments transferred to Luton. The head office was moved to 99, Queen Victoria Street, London. In 1905 Hayward Tyler & Co became a Private Limited Company after one of the directors' future father-in-law did not wish his daughter to be put at financial risk should the company fold.

The new century also saw Hayward Tyler & Co concentrating on pumps and pumping ancillary equipment and lessening their reliance on mineral water machinery and sanitary ware. This change in emphasis was largely due to the development by the company of a unique design of electric motor. In 1908 Mr W R MacDonald succeeded in winding an electric motor with rubber cable and operating it under water. The motor stator, which encases the cable, was filled with water which cooled the cable and lubricated the bearings. Hayward Tyler & Co came to an agreement with Mr MacDonald that this motor design be incorporated in their marine salvage pumps for which the British Admiralty became the principal customer.

The borehole submersible motor/pump was developed from this design by Mr Reed Cooper in 1930 and is now used by many water companies in the UK and overseas. Hayward Tyler

Luton Fire Station circa 1903

& Co has manufactured this type of unit in the elongated form since that time, with motor powers ranging from 15kw up to 2,000kw. With the submersible unit the motor and pump are coupled together and lowered into the water borehole, sometimes to depths of many hundreds of feet.

After the 2nd World War there was an insatiable thirst for power, be it for heavy machinery for industry or small domestic items for single houses. There was an urgent need for new electricity generating power stations. Hayward Tyler engineers foresaw a demand for pumps able to circulate water in boiler systems operating at pressures of many hundreds or even thousands of lbs/square inch and water temperatures in excess of 600 degrees Fahrenheit. They carried out experiments using the submersible motor and pump design encased inside a high pressure steel forged vessel. The experiments were a complete success with two motor/pumps being built and, after service on the boiler, stripped down. The units were carefully examined but no sign of wear or damage found. The designs were at once put in hand for larger and more ambitious motor/pumps.

The first customer was the American government who placed an order for two units to operate at pressures of up to 4,000 lbs/square inch. They were for a secret project, probably the nuclear industry. The units were well suited for this environment as motor and pump are in one sealed container with zero leakage. These pumps were first used in the UK at Calder Hall Nuclear Power Station and 32 Hayward Tyler glandless units were specified. These glandless motor/pumps became the standard equipment for nuclear and fossil fuel stations in many countries throughout the world.

In 1976 Hayward Tyler acquired the firm Sumo Pumps Ltd, manufacturers of dry stator borehole submersible motor/pump units. These units fitted into the lower duty end of the market where competition was keener and batch production methods used. In view of this a factory was set up in Keighley, Yorkshire and became a successful part of the organisation.

By 1983 Hayward Tyler had manufacturing and marketing facilities in the USA, Holland and Italy, together with a large network of agents throughout the world.

Today Hayward Tyler Ltd are involved in supplying equipment to three main industries –

(A) High Pressure Boiler Water Circulating Pumps for the Power Industry

(B) Pumps and Motors for the Off-shore Oil and Gas Industry

(C) Seal-less Pumps for the Oil Process Industry.

Oil Process Pumps and Submersible Motor/Pumps are still manufactured to order.

Mr Hayward Tyler, I believe, would be surprised and proud to know that the company, of which he was the proprietor all those years ago in London, still bears his name into the 21st Century.

Hayward Tyler Animal Power

Hayward Tyler & Co not only manufactured High Tech Pumps but also Low Tech ones. In 1923 they purchased the licence to manufacture a range of Noria Pumps from W & C Burgess of Animal Driven Pumps. These pumps were normally for the Middle or Far East market.

To calculate the output of this type of pump certain facts must be taken into account, firstly the type of animals available to drive the pumps.

For example:

(A) A Bullock will walk at 1.5 miles per hour over an 8 hour day.

(B) Three Bullocks equal the strength of two horses.

(C) A Horse will walk at 2.5 miles per hour over an 8 hour day.

(D) A Mule will walk at 2.5 miles per hour over an 8 hour day, although its strength is only equal to that of one Bullock.

(E) An Ass or Donkey will walk at 1.5 miles per hour, but its

IMPROVED WATER LIFT OR NORIA

FOR ONE OR MORE BULLOCKS, HORSES, OR MULES

PRIZE MEDAL AT THE CALCUTTA EXHIBITION, 1884   *Code*—LUCIUS

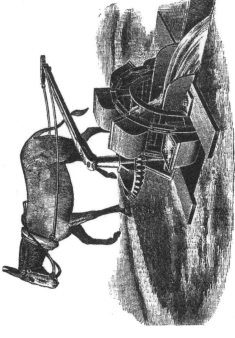

The above illustration shows a No. 0 or 1, worked by a Mule

These Water-Lifts, or Bucket Pumps, have been used for many years in India, Egypt, Cape Colony, etc., and are the simplest machines, as well as the most efficient for the purpose, raising considerably more water for the power applied than any other form of Pump. No fixing is required ; the machine is merely placed level over the well, which may be round or rectangular, or on a stage projecting from the bank of a canal or river, and the chain and buckets hang into the water, and may be lengthened as the water sinks. The quantity that may be raised depends upon depth and the power available.

In many parts of India it is usual to work with two bullocks yoked together, and in that case the bullocks walk in front of the draught pole, and the yoke is connected with the end of the pole by a piece of chain passing between the bullocks. For prices and particulars see following page.

Water Lift Pump worked by a Mule

strength is only one third of that of a Bullock.

(F) When a pump is worked by Horses or Mules, the flow of water is half as much again compared with that of Bullocks.

The pump outputs were based on Bullocks, with corrections made for other animals

For example:

A pump powered by one Bullock would lift 4,000 gallons per hour of water to a height of 20ft.

Two Bullocks would lift 6,000 gallons per hour of water to a height of 20ft.

Three Bullocks would lift 6,000 gallons per hour of water to a height of 40ft.

Four Bullocks would lift 6,000 gallons per hour of water to a height of 60ft.

When James Watt wanted to give his customers an idea of how powerful his steam engines were, he rated them in horse power. He calculated that one horse could do 33,000 ft/lbs of work per minute. In fact the average horse can only do 22,000 ft/lbs of work per minute. Watt's customers, well aware of the strength of their horses, were well satisfied with the power produced by his engines.

NB One horse equals the strength of five men.

Colin Cook 2003

LARGE SIZED WATER LIFT PUMP

Fitted with two barrels to be worked by two or more Bullocks, Horses or Mules

This illustration shows the arrangement for 3 Bullocks. If yoked in pairs 4, 6 or 8 Bullocks can be attached, as shown in the illustration of Cotton Gin worked by Bullocks (see back). When ordering, the number of poles required should be stated.

Large Water Lift Pump

Chapter 4

Into The Fens

In 1954 I, with my three friends, Ernie, Keith and Mick, felt it was time we had a holiday with a difference. Aged 18 we had been out to work for three years still going on family holidays and we wanted to experience a holiday on our own. After much discussion we decided that we would hire a motor cruiser and explore the Fens, a modern day Hereward the Wake.

First we obtained a map of the Fens and were surprised how large the area was. The nearest starting place for us in the Luton area would be Cambridge and we could hire a boat from there.

We contacted H C Banham Ltd, Riverside Works, Cambridge who were sited on the River Cam and had a list of holiday craft for hire. Banham's kindly sent to us

Colin with Keith

Ernie Cockburn and Keith Halstead

their catalogue, together with full details of the area, rates and conditions of hire and full details of each boat.

The catalogue was read cover to cover a few times. We were now in a position to book a suitable boat, and the forms and cheque were completed. It was all systems go, with three months to make arrangements and lay plans.

At last the day of our trip arrived and plans were put into effect. We travelled to Hitchin by bus, then by train to Cambridge and taxi to the boatyard. Banham's fleet

Mick Taylor

MAP OF NAVIGABLE RIVERS
OF CAMBRIDGESHIRE

Map of the Fens

consisted of approximately 30 boats. The proper time to join the boat was from 4.00pm Saturday, and all craft must be given up by 10.00am on the next Saturday. The boat we had hired was a four berth cruiser named Caprice, at a cost of £17 per week, plus a 10 foot sailing dinghy at £2 per week.

The catalogue details of the boat were as follows - "Really delightful small double-cabin boat. Length 25ft, beam (width) 8ft. Each cabin has two single spring berths, drawers under. Separate space with WC and wash-basin. Galley with sink and Calor gas cooking. Cabin has raised centre with sliding windows for ventilation. Head-room 5ft 10ins to 6ft. Morris 4-cylinder

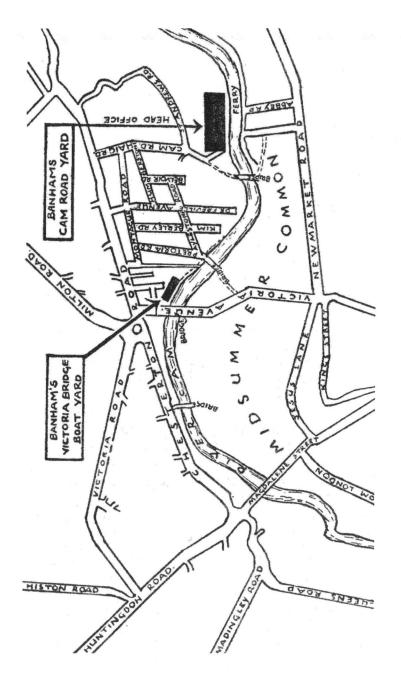

Banham's Boatyard in Cambridge

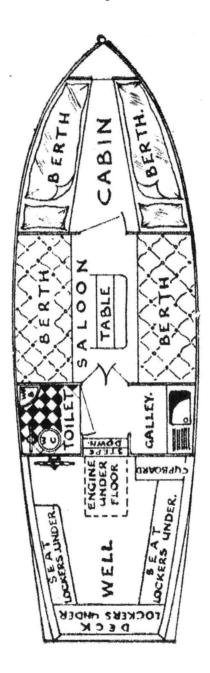

Caprice

self starter marine engine fitted under well floor. Wheel steering with controls brought to a handy position. Electric light. Fresh-water tank. All usual requisites for four persons, except towels and linen."

The boatyard was organised chaos, with sailing boats and motorised cruisers coming in, berthing, changing crews and going out again. As we had time to spare before picking up the boat, we went to the nearest shops to stock up on food, toiletries and a **few** cans of beer. After the formalities at the boatyard we were given a half hour instruction in nautical ways and local terms of endearment. Then, tethering the dinghy to the stern (nautical word for the back of the boat), we were ready for the off. Our instructor waved goodbye "see you next Saturday" and the engine was started (starter motor, no handle).

The cry went up "let go forward, let go aft". The engine gave a throaty hum, the gear lever was put in forward mode, the friend at the wheel said "slow ahead", the boat slipped its moorings and we moved into the river channel, the compass read due north and our adventure holiday had begun.

For the next week the pace of life would be 4 mph, the recommended boat speed. Our first objective was getting through Baitsbite Lock before the light went. The distance from the boatyard was 3 miles, which we covered in three quarters of an hour. The lock was open to us and we slowly edged forward. We were the only boat in the lock, so we moored as close as possible to the closed gate, lowered the fenders, held onto the forward and aft ropes and awaited the lock-keeper's instructions.

The lock-keeper was a most amenable man in, I judge, his early fifties. He gave much practical advice to us greenhorns of the river and told us how dangerous the locks could be. He was pleased to see that the fore and aft mooring ropes were hand held and not tied to the back wall. As he explained, water will quickly enter the locks when the gates were opened and the depth of the water changes by eight feet or more in a few

APPROXIMATE CRUISING TIMES

From	To	Approx time taken
Cambridge	Baitsbite	30 mins
"	Clayhithe	50 mins
"	Bottisham	1 hr
"	Upware	1 hr 30 mins
"	Old West River	2 hrs
"	Ely	2 hrs 30 mins
Ely	River Lark	40 mins
"	Littleport	1 hr
"	Ship Inn	1 hr 30 mins
"	River Wissey	2 hrs 10 mins
"	Denver	2 hrs 25 mins
River Lark		
Entrance	Prickwillow	25 mins
(Branch Bridge)	Isleham Lock	1 hr 35 mins
"	Judes Ferry Bridge	2 hrs
Brandon Creek		
Entrance	Little Ouse Bridge	20 mins
(Ship Inn)	Green Dragon	1 hr 10 mins
"	Wilton Bridge	1 hr 50 mins
River Wissey		
Entrance	Hilgay Bridge	25 mins
"	Wissington Beet Factory	1 hr
"	Stoke Ferry Bridge	1 hr 45 mins
	Old West River	
Fish & Duck Inn	Stretham Bridge	35 mins
"	Twenty Pence Bridge	1 hr
"	Hermitage Lock	2 hrs 25 mins
	River Ouse	
Hermitage Lock	Brownshill Staunch	20 mins
"	Holywell	45 mins
"	St Ives Lock	1 hr 20 mins
"	Hemingford Lock	1 hr 45 mins
"	Houghton Lock	2 hrs
"	Godmanchester Lock	2 hrs 45 mins
"	Brampton Lock	3 hrs
"	Offord Lock	3 hrs 30 mins
"	Paxton Paper Mill Lock	4 hrs 30 mins
"	Eaton Socon Lock	5 hrs
"	Tempsford Bridge	5 hrs 40 mins

Above times do not include time taken going through locks.
On the River Ouse this may equal the cruising times.

minutes. Therefore you must be ready to pay out the ropes or take up the slack at once to prevent the boat from striking the lock walls or other boats with more than a little bump, or even tipping the boat if tied to the lock wall. We took this information to memory and realised how useful the fenders are. The lock-keeper also pointed out to us the sliding doors fitted into the lock gates. These were to control the flow of water in and out of the lock and should always be closed when not in use. In operation the doors are closed when the water level in the lock equals the level of the canal section you are about to enter and only then should you open the lock gates. If the sliding doors became jammed he told us to get help or a section of the canal would drain.

When we were ready to leave the lock, we thanked the keeper and gave him half-a-crown instead of the usual shilling. Information is priceless.

On leaving Baitsbite we made our way to Bottisham Lock which was a distance of 3 miles, and we decided to moor this side of the lock overnight at Clayhythe, as the light was fading fast and we had sleeping arrangements to make. The forward cabin was the smaller of the two, so the smallest members of the crew, Keith and I, took this. The other two bunks were in the saloon cabin and doubled as seats for meals. We were all Boys Brigade members, so simple cooking and light housework were second nature. After breakfast we passed through Bottisham Lock without any problems and then headed for Ely.

After leaving Bottisham Lock we enter the Fens proper. You do not notice this straight away as the river passes through high banks on either side, then suddenly your perspective increases like exiting a rail tunnel. The space is overwhelming and you are conscious of being alone in a silent and vast world.

The Fens are described by some as a flat, empty, featureless landscape, even desolate. Since the drainage of the Fens began in the 17th century trees and bushes have been encouraged. The

Fens are crisscrossed by long straight drains named by their width, for example Twenty Foot Drain. These have been dug over the centuries in an effort to control frequent flooding, and the not so frequent droughts, and to provide water for irrigation of this vast land.

Early Drainage of the Fens

In the early 17th century the Earl of Bedford employed the Dutch engineer Vermuyden to drain part of the Fens in order to create land for agriculture. The peat, when drained, quickly dries out and begins to shrink, resulting in a fall in the ground level. This can be up to the height of a man in his lifetime. Over the years it was necessary from time to time to pump rainwater from the fields up and into the rivers which had remained at the pre-drainage levels. The design of pump used to drain the Fens was a wind powered scoop pump (low lift, high volume). So windmills became a feature of the Fenland scene. These had scoop wheels with paddles set at an angle of about 30 degrees and were made to rotate in a channel cut in the peat or brick lined. By the speed of rotation water can be efficiently raised to one fifth of the wheel's diameter. With wind being the motive power, 25 feet is the practical maximum diameter for scoop wheels and a lift of 3 feet for best efficiency.

The majority of scoop wheels are designed for a peripheral speed of 5 to 8 feet per second at a speed of 4 revolutions per minute. The ideal wind speed would be 4 to 7 miles per hour. However, as we know, the wind is very unreliable and too often as the water level rose the wind pump stood idle due to lack of wind.

The early part of the 19th century saw the introduction of steam driven pumps which gave a control over drainage and volumes pumped. Pump powers increased from a few horsepower up to hundreds. Centrifugal pumps superseded the scoop wheel. Many pumps now are diesel driven or electric. Today many crops are grown on the Fens and in some places sheep and cattle raised.

Our first view of the Fens gave an eerie, white mist which was about 6 inches from the ground, looking like a calm sea, with Ely Cathedral in the distance and reminding us of an island rising out of the mist, only to vanish again when the mist enveloped it.

Journeying on our way towards Ely we pass on our right Swaffam and Bottesham Lodes which, due to their width and depth, are only navigable for dinghies. The vast roof of the "Lord Nelson" in Upware now comes into view. This inn bears the sign on its gable end "Five Miles From Anywhere, No Hurry".

Burwell Lode, although only about four miles long, is worth a visit but, as this is our first day in the Fens, we decided to come back later on in the week when we would be more relaxed. On our left we pass the entrance into the Old West River which flows from the Cam to the Ouse, with a brief view of the Stretham Engine House. The junction of the Cam and Old West Rivers is called Pope's Corner and is the site of the Fish and Duck Inn (they serve a good pint). On our first Fenland holiday the Old West River was generously endowed with water, however in dry summers you are well advised to keep to the middle of the river to prevent scraping the bottom of the boat. We proceeded to Ely and were surprised at the abundance of wildlife; animals, birds and vegetation. The river bends and we get a breathtaking view of Ely Cathedral, with its West Tower rising 215 feet from the flat, almost bare landscape of the Fens.

Arriving at Ely, we moor at the quayside which adjoins Appleyards Boathouse, and take on petrol and water. Afterwards we walked into the city to do some exploration and pick up some provisions. Shopping completed, we return to the boat, taking note that early closing is on Tuesdays.

Just past Ely on the river there is a large Sugarbeet Factory, but care must be taken when passing one of the beet barges, especially if the barge has several others in tow. Due to the bends on the canal or river, it is sometimes difficult to navigate some bends without the swinging end barge grazing one of the banks. The barge skippers will generally advise you about the best side on which to pass.

Five miles on from Ely on the right-hand side, we come to the junction with the River Lark. Four miles up this river is the hamlet of Prickwillow and the site of Prickwillow Drainage Pumping Engine.

In this way we proceeded northwards along the Great Ouse River (the river changed its name from the Cam once we had left Ely), investigating every inlet and creek including the River Wissey and Brandon Creek, both navigable for four miles from the Ouse. Eventually rounding the bend in the Ouse, we came face to face with Denver Sluice, the point at which the Ouse changes from the non-tidal to the tidal river. Denver Sluice is the key to the drainage and irrigation of the Fens, incorporating the Bedford River, the Great Ouse and the drainage river of the South and East Levels.

Before setting off, we had been strongly advised by Banham's staff not to enter the tidal rivers. Looking at Denver Sluice and consulting the map we felt that even with the maximum time available between tides it would be difficult to circumnavigate the Isle of Ely and get back to the safety of Hermitage Lock before the tide changed leaving us high and dry. So it was with some reluctance that we retraced our journey and returned to Ely.

The next morning we left Ely, travelled south down the Cam and entered the Old West River after ¾ hour of cruising and wound our way along it to Hermitage Lock, a distance of 10 miles, two and a half hours of cruising. On the way we passed Stretham Engine House on our left. The Stretham Steam Engine was built in 1831 when ten or so other engines were at work with a total power of 436 bhp. The Level Commissioners had awarded the contract for the engine's two boilers and scoop wheels at a cost of £2,900 to Mr Joseph Glynn. Mr Glynn worked for the Butterley Company who supplied all the ironwork for this engine. Incidentally, the Butterley Company supplied the ironwork roofing supports for the main arches at St Pancras mainline railway station. The engine boiler pressure was between three and four pounds per square inch, which was the maximum possible with the older type of boiler. Later, in 1888, the pressure was increased to eight pounds per square inch.

Apart from the rivers Cam and Ouse, the main waterways in the area of the Fens are mostly created by man and go by the fancy names such as the Twenty Foot and Sixteen Foot Drain. That was why we found the Old West River a joy to cruise, linking the Cam to the Ouse, following its twists and turns and wondering what awaits around the next corner. It was an ideal stretch of water to hone our tacking skills in the dinghy avoiding being blown into the onshore bank. In next to no time we reach Hermitage Lock and, after checking that the dinghy is still with us, we bear left into the Ouse.

The distance from Hermitage Lock to St Ives is 5½ miles, which we covered in one and a half hours. We were able to moor at the quay in the town centre and decided to stay the night. St Ives is a pretty country town with an attractive old stone bridge crossing the river close to the town centre. Attractive arches support this bridge built in the middle ages, with a chapel in the bridge centre. When we arrived at St Ives it was already dusk, so mooring was uppermost in our minds. We decided to go underneath one of the arches, turn round and moor. The river was running high, so we decided to go underneath the larger arch close to the chapel and lined up the boat. It was not until we were close to the bridge that we realised the boat was riding too high. Someone shouted "Everybody Down!" and the boat hit with a sickening thud. That night we were in a sombre mood, waiting for morning to survey the damage.

We arose early next morning and I remembered Mum's

advice, "things don't look half so bad in the cold light of day" and she was right. The damage was only slight and a visit to St Ives' hardware shop provided all the necessary wood and tools. Thank goodness for our woodwork classes at school. After our endeavours at restoration and a well earned lunch, we weighed anchor and set a course for St Neots.

This 16½ mile stretch is my favourite length of the Great Ouse, as there are a number of small towns and waterways to explore and locks to experience. There are also a number of historic churches and enough wildlife to keep Bill Oddie occupied all summer. We took out the dinghy and honed our sailing skills, which paved the way for a future open boat holiday the next year. After leaving St Neots, we went down to Eaton Socon Lock, which at that time was the limit of navigable water. Nowadays it is possible to take the cruise down to Bedford.

It suddenly dawned upon us that it was now Thursday night and the boat had to be back at Cambridge by 10 o'clock on Saturday morning. We made very good time on Friday, passing through the locks like professional canal boatmen. The week on the Fens was a holiday which stayed with us a long time, teaching us a range of new skills.

Will we come back to the Fens? Yes, why, because it is now in our blood. Dawn in the Fens must be experienced; a way of life I thought was gone for ever.

Colin Cook 2005

Chapter 5

Memories of Ruby

Why should 40 years be a bench mark? On the approach of my 40th birthday I, like countless others have done, sat down for a spell of reflection on my life so far. I realised I had been fortunate in having a loving supportive wife, two fine boys anyone would be proud of, a good job and many interests. However, I felt I needed a new challenge. In my teens I had owned with a friend a three wheeler Morgan sports car, and the memory and dream of having an old car was still fresh in my mind. To turn a dream into reality can cause some problems, especially if it's impractical, expensive and selfish. My dream was to own a pre 1939-1945 Austin Ten or Seven car.

After seeking and obtaining my wife's support, I then began to solve the practicalities of the venture. First and foremost was the question of accommodation. The Austin would, of course, have to be housed in the garage. This meant that a carport would need to be built for the family car. From the first drawing for planning and building permission to the completion and passing of the 26 feet by 8 feet carport took the majority of 1976. The carport turned into a project of its own, with planning and costing, bills of materials and council planning approval. I had to set a plan of action. The area in consideration was the sideway between the house and the boundary fence from the garage to the house hallway window, which was also the extent of the boundary fence. This encased an area of 26 feet long and 8 feet wide. From this point to the pavement is open plan.

The height of the carport was fixed in that the carport roof must be higher than the top of the house side door and below the waste water and drain down-pipe wall fixings. This gave a gap of 6 to 7 inches wide for fixing the main carport beam to the wall of the house, the gap between the wall and the down-pipe being 2½ inches. This gave me the main beam section of 6 inches by 2 inches. The boundary fence of the carport would be supported by 4 scaffolding poles, and on the top of each a tee shaped support. The horizontal tee arms supported the main beam on the boundary side and these slid into the top of the scaffolding poles. Spacer washers were placed between the scaffolding poles and the tee pieces to ensure that the beam was firmly supported at each pole. This arrangement made up for any unevenness in the sideway concrete base. The scaffolding poles were let into the sideway base by chiselling out four 3 inch diameter holes 9 inches deep. The concrete was unbelievably hard and it took its toll on my chisels and my bruised fingers. It was at the height of summer in 1976, a very hot summer, which meant an early morning start while the temperature was comparatively cool. The cross beams, 8 in number and 4 inches by 2 inches in section, strengthened the carport frame and supported the corrugated plastic roof. Plastic guttering and pipes were then fitted to the boundary side of the carport which completed the work. I cannot believe that this work took all summer, however it was now completed and I returned to the main task of finding an old car.

During this time I was making enquiries through the Austin Ten Club, which I had joined in the middle of 1976, and reading the Exchange and Mart to get a feeling of prices and conditions. By September I was ready to try in earnest to obtain a suitable

Ruby under the Carport

Ruby under the Carport

car. I followed up three or four possibilities, experiencing gazumping on two occasions, until finally I saw an Austin Seven Ruby advertised at Orpington and, after a telephone call to the seller, an antique dealer, I went down to see the car.

The car was an Austin Seven Ruby Saloon built in September 1936, five months after I was born. Pure Art Deco fitted with a sun roof, wire spoke wheels, a hinged windscreen for increased ventilation and powered by a 750cc side valve engine, all the electrics being 6 volts. It was housed in a garage, but looking dusty and forlorn. We pushed it out in the open and I began to have a look round and noted there were no doors (these were still in the garage without glass); the running boards on both sides all but dropping off the car; the interior in a bad state; upholstery virtually non existent; wings dented and split.

I was a little disappointed to say the least, but the chassis was in good condition, so was the engine, also the body, albeit dented in places. "It's all there," said the man. "Just like an Airfix kit; would you like a ride?" Well, after coming all that way, I could only say yes.

The ride was quite an experience, sitting on a doggy seat in a car with no doors, but she handled well and the engine sounded sweet. So on balance I felt it was worth a go, and after a little discussion, we agreed a price. The Austin was mine.

Two days later a small car transporter appeared outside our house with my Austin on top, looking sad and forlorn. I had my doubts and quickly pushed it into the garage, away from prying eyes. The first step was to check that all the parts were there, all unfixed parts being inside the car. I then gave the car a good clean inside and out.

The next job was to put the windows in place in the doors and hang both of them. This, as is always the case, took much longer than I dare admit. Next I decided to begin underneath the car at the back, cleaning, repairing and painting as I went. It was an unbelievably dirty but satisfying job, not to be tackled by those suffering with rheumatism; I have never been so stiff in all my life. I was surprised to find that most of the car was held together by nuts and bolts, with very little welding. The wings were next, splits being repaired with resin. The whole underneath was then painted.

The engine compartment was in good condition, only requiring a cleaning and lick of paint. Then, to the running boards, which were in a poor state. Reinforcing with stainless steel plate was necessary to give strength to the body. On all repairs I used nuts and bolts, so keeping to the original design.

The complete inside of the car was then stripped out, wire brushed and where necessary painted. Then the tricky part: the re-trim. I had to make hardboard templates of the inside of the car doors and cover them with vinyl. The doors were now completed and I then had to re-cover the seats, stuffing them with foam, as they were originally pneumatic. My wife helped me to line the inside of the car with vinyl; we did our best but it was not strictly authentic, as our skills and finances were limited.

I then turned my attention to the braking and steering systems, renewing where necessary. The exhaust pipe was in surprisingly good condition, and even after 29 years of owning the car, the exhaust never needed replacing or repairing. Worn electrical parts were replaced and a new wiring loom fitted. The advantage in owning an Austin Seven is that all spares are readily available.

Bodywork was next on the list, followed by a re-spray. A friend's father re-sprayed the car for me for the cost of two bottles of whisky. The main body was sprayed in a deep red ruby colour with black wings. New tyres had to be sourced, as the original ones showed great signs of wear.

When all this work was completed, it was the spring of 1980. The rebuild of the car had taken nearly three and a half years, on and off. How time goes when you are having fun.

Now I had to put all my work on the Austin to the test and put it in for its MOT. The car, as I had anticipated, failed its first test.

Ruby at one of the first Car Rallies

Ruby in the Show Ring

The brakes were not up to the required standard and this meant stripping down the brakes and readjusting the brake wires and levers until the required readings on all wheels was achieved. It passed the next MOT with flying colours. The brakes on the car are all cable operated and after each trip need attention to regain the required standard, ensuring that all brakes come on at the same time to prevent skids, instability and loss of control. I had gone to a few Steam and Car Rallies at this time and at one of these met up with two car enthusiasts who explained to me the rally scene; they were Frank Whayman and Alex Croft and with their guidance and enthusiasm I entered my Austin Seven Ruby in the Welwyn Garden City Rally in September 1980. There began my rallying career which spanned over 26 years and with my wife and, in early days my sons too, I attended nearly 200 events. During this time we covered over 10,500 miles in the car, which was only off the road for a few weeks, while having new piston rings fitted and a new front leaf-spring.

The car proved very reliable over this period, with only two punctures and a carburettor screw working loose. Now and again, after Winter's inclement weather the car, having stood a few months in the garage, was reluctant to start in the Spring. I found out this was usually due to the condenser. This involved a call to the AA on our Home Start Cover and they connected the Austin up to a 12 volt battery which started the car straight away. This exercise was repeated a few times over the 26 years. The AA men always enjoyed this immensely. I am pleased to say this was the only regular problem.

Each time we went out in the Ruby I was very aware of the limitations of the car, especially when I had my wife and two boys on board. With performance 0 to 40 miles an hour in a few minutes, brakes being all cable operated and showing slow response and the first two gears in the gearbox being crash gears, which called for fancy footwork while I attempted to execute a double declutch, meant driving with extreme care and attention.

A satisfied AA Man

Ready for the Bridesmaids at a friend's wedding

The car had a very small rear window which could be a problem on motorways. There is, however, one advantage in driving a slow, old car; you nearly always have the open road in front of you, even though you have many frustrated car drivers behind.

Unfortunately, due to failing health, I could no longer maintain or drive the car, and so in 2005 I reluctantly allowed a friend to advertise the car on the Internet. To my surprise I received a telephone call from Spain from a man who wished to purchase the car as a surprise Christmas present for his stepfather who lived near Ely and had recently retired. So, two days before Christmas 2005, a friend of his arrived with a low-loader and, after inspecting the car, we did a deal and Ruby went out of my life. A few days later the new owner telephoned me to say how pleased he was with the car and was looking forward to working on her and rallying her himself, so I know she has gone to a good home not too far away. Looking back on my time with the Austin Seven Ruby, it was a wonderful period in my life, a chance to drive an icon of British motoring while meeting many interesting people.

Colin Cook 2006

Displaying the Rally Plaques

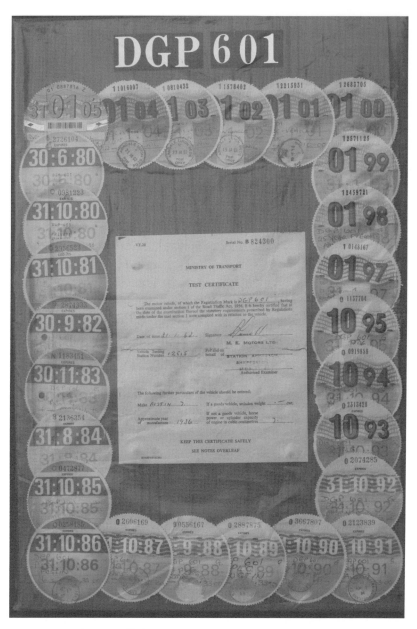

Displaying all the Tax Discs and first MOT Certificate

Chapter 6

A Visit to a Hat Factory

*E*ven in Luton we refer to the hat industry in the past tense, as though it is in terminal decline. It is true that there are fewer factories than was the case prior to the 2nd World War; those that remain, however, are buoyant, forward looking and facing the 21st Century with confidence. Of course in an industry which is fashion led there are inevitably changes. Manufacturers must always be aware of trends in clothing and seasonal colours. Luton hats are international and have many customers overseas whose fashions do not necessarily mirror the UK.

In February 2002 I was given the opportunity to visit the hat manufacturers S G Parker & Sons (Luton) Ltd of Collingdon Street, Luton established in 1898 and was hosted on a guided tour by the owner Mr Roger Parker.

The premises were originally a typical 19th Century middle class town house with ground floor bay windows and steps up to the front door. Most of the rooms of the house are retained, some with the original cast iron fire places. The rear main room, which would have looked into the back yard and garden, still retains the bay window ledge and iron railings, although this area which once led to the carriage house and stable is now covered in to form an extension to the factory. The hallway is

S G Parker & Sons, Collingdon Street, Luton

original, with an attractive arch and floor tiles. A large cellar, which was strengthened to form an air raid shelter during the war, was the kitchen and still has the floor tiles. The original inside water closet is still in use as the men's toilet, although the ornate ceramic pan was broken recently whilst being removed for restoration.

The tour started on the first floor where the fabric is stored for the manufacture of the brims and crowns in a host of colours and shades. One fabric is a natural plant fibre called Sinamay. Only a small proportion of hats these days are made from felt or straw. For the majority of us, hats are not worn as part of our daily attire, being reserved for social engagements such as weddings and garden parties. Sinamay is from the Phillipines and comes from the Abacca tree which is the same family as the banana tree. Sinamay, being a natural fibre, can present problems in dyeing, as the fibre texture may vary from batch to batch, and even in a single batch, which could affect the final shade.

In one of the first floor rooms are the milliners, a group of ladies responsible for adding the adornments and finishing touches to the hats. This generally means hand sewing, and ranges from a trimming of a simple band, to a more elaborate process of veiling, drapes and/or flowers. These ladies are the inside miiiiners and work closely with the designers in the next room, experimenting how a particular design works, in ease of manufacture, time taken, and cost of materials. Another

Displaying Hats in the Office

group of milliners work in their own homes; boxes of basic hats together with the necessary materials and cottons and instructions, not forgetting a sample finished hat, are delivered weekly and the finished hats collected. These outside milliners are paid according to the number of hats correctly produced to the sample. Millinery is very skilled work calling for speed and dexterity. It is not easy for hat manufacturers to find skilled workers, as nowadays sewing is rarely taught at home or in the schools, so good workers are highly prized. Sometimes the hat boxes will be sent many miles to a first class milliner.

We then moved on to the cutting room where the varieties of materials are cut to shape from dimensions given on the job card or from a template. The large cutting tables, round chalk and large scissors have similarities to a bespoke tailor's work room where equivalent skills are required to ensure exactness of cut with the minimum of waste. All these jobs are carried out with swiftness and deceptive ease.

The blocking machines, because of their weight, are situated on the ground floor. From the design for the hat shape a plaster mould is made before an aluminium shape is cast, which is known as a block, and is generally made in two pieces. The block is set on the blocking machine and heated, usually by gas, to the correct temperature for the material used. Blocking is a process of stretching various different materials over the hot block shapes using steam to soften them. Materials are held in place with a blocking cord to prevent creasing. This process is performed by people known as Blockers who will block up to 100 hats a day using five or six different shapes. It is from this that the basic hat shape is formed.

Different materials are blocked in slightly different ways. Sisal and Parasisal hoods are from China and are either cone shaped or have crown and brim together. These are blocked on the Gas Pans and finished on Hydraulic Blocking Machines or, if a simple shape, just put straight into the Hydraulic Blocking

Gas Blocking Machines

Machines. Hydraulics are used as, by using water pressure, they can give gentle or high pressure as required. Felt and straw hats are blocked from a cone shape known as a hood. The straw is generally stiffened with a lacquer before it is blocked to give a lasting shape, whereas the felt contains a proofing. Other materials such as polyesters and satin are laid into flat squares with buckram, a bonding and stiffening material, in between two pieces, with the crown and brim being blocked separately.

The machinist room is also on the ground floor; here wire is machined on to the edge of the hat brim to hold it in shape. A Petersham, leather, rayon or silk band is sewn inside the crown to give the correct head fit. Bindings of ribbon can be machined onto the edge of the brim; crowns and brims can be swapped around to give alternative shapes and contrasting colours. The machines used are specifically designed for each operation; some fitted with a sewing needle, others with a knife for cutting. Machines used in the Hat Industry are unique and cannot easily

Hydraulic Blocking Machines – the old ones are steam heated and the modern one in the foreground is electrical

A 17 Guinea Sewing Machine

Hat Machinists at work

be replaced; they are, however, of robust construction, some being over 100 years old and still performing well.

The despatch department is an extremely busy part of the organisation, for hat boxes, although light, are very bulky and take up a large amount of room. Some boxes are for sending out to the outside milliners, others for sending to United Kingdom customers or overseas. In each case contents must be carefully checked against the paperwork. Space in the department is always at a premium, so delays must be kept at a minimum.

I wish to thank Mr Roger Parker for an interesting and instructive tour.

Colin Cook 2003

S G Parker and Sons, Hat Manufacturers closed down in 2005 when Mr Roger Parker retired.

Chapter 7

A Walk from Luton to Biscot

Come with me now on a journey of the mind. It is at the turn from the 19th to the 20th Century and there is a keen wind this fine October afternoon as we start a walk to Biscot. We are starting from George Street, Luton and make our way past a large number of horse drawn carts laden with hat boxes, taking hats from the factories down Bute Street and on to the railway stations.

Our walk takes us down Manchester Street, formerly called Tower Hill and into the aristocratic area of New Bedford Road, and then across the Great Moor where we pick up the lane to Biscot (later called Biscot Road) and soon are at the end of the row of houses on the outskirts of the north side of the town of Luton. The lane gently rises so that you may see the New Bedford Road below and the Bramingham Shott Estate, later to be called Wardown. This will be a perfect park for a people's playground, well wooded and easily accessible, but it is some way from the town. The lane now becomes a path between arable fields, and passing a large corn-rick we see farm-hands gathering the remaining corn and a little beyond a farmer's cart ready to convey their burdens to the rick. In the distance, on the ridge, stands Biscot Windmill, keeping watch over the fields and looking somewhat bleak in the watery sun. We do not know how long ago it was when the first mill stood on this site, but the pasture on which it stands is known as Mill Field (Millfield Road).

From the ridge the land to the east falls gently down to the River Lea at a spot called Stockingstone (the boundary between the parishes of Biscot and Stopsley); the ground then rises steeply to Cowridge and on to Round Green. To the west the path joins the Icknield Way and on to Dunstable. Our way is north down a steep path (now called St Margarets Avenue) to the right of the mill down to the village of Biscot nestling under the lee of the ridge. The path once called Limbury Road is now Bishopscote Road. On entering Biscot village, we follow a large imposing wall which encloses the gardens and vicarage of Holy Trinity Church and follow the wall into Church Road (now Trinity Road) and note the sweeping entrance to the imposing late Victorian vicarage.

The stables, incorporating horses and carriages built at the same time as the church and vicarage, are to our right, separating the Vicarage from the churchyard. We would have been drawn to the stables by the sound of a whistling young stable lad at work sweeping the hay. We watch him at work, when he suddenly stops whistling and looks directly at us; he senses something is there, but we are from the future and he cannot see us. After a minute or so he smiles to himself and continues with his work, but the whistling is not so carefree. (This building with modifications is now the current church hall.) The original door to the hay loft can still be seen above our heads. The hay loft would possibly have housed the stable lad. In later times it became a den for the youth club. The stables had windows much smaller than those seen today, and therefore a fan-light was placed in the roof; this has always been a problem with rain water finding a way in, and creating difficulty in darkening the room for slide shows.

Biscot Churchyard

The large churchyard at Biscot gives the Church its rural setting, the total area being close on four acres. Its fauna and flora have been mentioned in the histories of Bedfordshire, although the habitat of wild life has to be weighed against the upkeep and maintenance of the churchyard. We may not have the very famous buried at Biscot, although each grave will yield a story for you to uncover. There are approximately 4,000 souls laying here and, although the churchyard is virtually closed, there are a few family spaces. In the past the churchyard served other churches in the area besides Anglican, and the trust set-up to administer the churchyard is represented from them.

Biscot Church

Walking on, we come to Biscot Church, which is dedicated to the Holy Trinity, the church and vicarage built by the Lord of

Biscot Church

the Manor of Biscot, John Sambrooke Crawley of Stockwood in 1868. The church is a pleasant and restrained example in the general trend of its day, when Gothic revival in the Early English Style was fashionable for ecclesiastical and school buildings. The use of bricks and stonework of contrasting colours was a characteristic of this architecture, as is exemplified by George Gilbert Scott's St Pancras Hotel which was being built at this time. It is interesting to note that the Leicestershire red sandstone used in the string courses and plinth in Biscot Church is the same as in that building. The building of the Midland Railway, commenced some four years before, had facilitated the transport of this material.

Biscot School
Biscot School stood next to the church on the other side of the churchyard. Built in 1876, it never was a church school, although it stood on land previously owned by Squire John Crawley, as originally did the church. A School Board was established in Luton in February 1874 after a long period of ignominious wrangling between the Anglican and Nonconformist bodies. The Revd E R Adams, Vicar of Holy Trinity Biscot, was a member of the board and, very unusual for the time, he was a Liberal. In Luton, Anglican vicars were, in the main, Conservatives, and Nonconformist ministers, Liberal. The elected School Board consisted of four Anglicans (known as the prayer book five), one of the five failing to be elected. There were four Nonconformists (known as the Bible five) plus the Vicar of Biscot who voted with the Bible five. The Revd E R Adams wanted a school built at Biscot and another at Leagrave, but he had been told by the Anglican authorities that the children should attend a school in Luton. This was unacceptable to Adams, who made an agreement with the Liberal members of the School Board that he would support them if they would agree to schools being built in Biscot and Leagrave. This saved the children a long

walk mornings and evenings. The additional schools at Biscot and Leagrave put an increase on the rates and made poor Adams the most unpopular member of the board. The school provided a primary education for children between the ages of 5 to 12 and accommodated 150 pupils in return for a few pence per week The school served the village for over 100 years before being demolished to make way for a West Indian Community Centre.

The Moat House at Biscot

After leaving Biscot Church we cross Trinity Road (previously called Church Road) and make our way down Nunnery Lane. In front of us where Nunnery Lane meets Moat Lane we would have seen the Tithe Barn and Village Pond, and also farm outhouses. These have now been demolished, leaving only Moat House farm which is now known as the Old Moat House, the oldest secular building in Luton, built sometime between 1370 and 1400. It is now a public house and restaurant.

The Moat House was a manor house up to the end of the 17th Century and then continued in occupation as a farm house through the 18th and 19th Centuries. It ceased to be inhabited in 1958 and its future became a matter of doubt and concern for those who care for local history.

After being acquired by Bedfordshire Council, with its preservation in mind it passed to the care of Luton Corporation on attainment of County Borough status. For the next few years it suffered considerably from vandal damage, including two fires and from the effects of neglect and decay. From the early 1970s its fortunes changed dramatically, and it is now a very popular meeting place restored to its former glory with a few sympathetic modifications.

Holy Trinity Church has a tangible connection with the Moat House in the shape of two iron chests which were found buried on the farm shortly after 1850. The land belonging as it did to Squire Crawley, they passed into his possession. One of the chests is now in Biscot Church and the other at Stockwood Museum. The chests which date from the early 17th Century were perhaps intended as deed boxes.

The original purpose of the Moat House has been the subject of some controversy over the years. Historians dispute over the roofing beams, which are of oak and of great strength, richly moulded; perhaps being a bit too fancy for a manor or farm house. This has led some to believe that this was a chapel roof, as writings state "There was formerly a considerable house for Nuns at Biscot founded by Roger, Abbot of St Albans, and dedicated to the Holy Trinity".

Frederick Davis in his "History of Luton" 1874 states, "At its dissolution this religious house was valued at £143-18s-3d". There are some portions of the original building still standing which now form part of the restaurant. It must have been a place of great strength and extent, as the walls still standing are very thick. At one end of the house are two strong buttresses of Totternhoe stone, evidently part of the original building. Some of the chimney pieces still remain; they are massive and built of the same stone. On one of the chimney pieces, deeply cut in capitals, is the following:- "There was hailstons fel 23rd July of this bignes and liknes. 1666. TF." One of the stones was circular, and measured no less than half an inch in diameter, the other was oval, and measured one inch in length.

The 1902 Year Book

From The Luton and District Year Book for 1902, Biscot with Limbury is described as a Village about two miles from Luton and one mile from Leagrave Station with a population of 400. The Board school is under the control of the Luton School Board, and has accommodation for 153 scholars. The head-mistress is Mrs Maidment, who is assisted by Misses Cowley, Ward, Glenister and Craig. The caretaker is Mrs M A Bass. The Overseers of the school are Messrs A Blundell and James

Smith; the Assistant Overseer and Parish Council Clerk is Mr G Maidment. During the winter a carpentry class is held under the auspices of the Beds County Council, Mr Maidment is the teacher. There is a flourishing Band of Hope with about 130 members; the meetings are held in the school and are conducted on unsectarian lines, the President is Mr Maidment. (It is clear that Mr and Mrs Maidment are well known figures in the life of Biscot.) There are two postal collections and two deliveries of letters each day, Sundays excepted.

Biscot in 1915

Aubrey S Darby, author of "A View from the Alley", spent a convalescing holiday in Biscot recovering from a peritonitis operation carried out at the Bute Hospital. From his book I gather that the year was 1915 and Aubrey would have been ten years old. Aubrey's mother had a distant relative who lived in the village of Biscot and this seemed an ideal location to convalesce. Aubrey recalled Biscot as being a small hamlet, comprising of two farms, Mr Craig farmed Moat Farm and Mr Hartops farmed Grange Farm. There was a pond in the road, a Parish church, a nearby school, and about fifty cottages mostly owned by the two farmers. The cottage where Aubrey stayed was in Moat Lane, one of a terraced row, and he recalled it was very small even when compared with his home in Princess Street. The cottage had no gas, electricity or piped water, the toilet being an earth closet thirty yards from the back door, and a communal well served the cottages. The young man he stayed with was a farm labourer and his wife a housewife come washerwoman.

There were no shops in Biscot at that time, so the villagers had to provide for themselves, obtaining dairy products and eggs from the farm, becoming experts in cooking and providing game for the table. Aubrey experienced a healthy diet and good country air, and, as he said, this was not rural poverty it was a rural paradise.

In Conclusion

After leaving Moat Farm we walk down a path called Moat Lane, passing two rows of terraced houses occupied by farm workers, and on to Meadow Lane where used to stand Grange Farm. The day is now nearly spent, so we make our way past Biscot Church and on to Limbury with its attractive Baptist Chapel, Manor and Farm, also the Black Swan Inn. Leagrave, with its rail station, is now in our sights and, as the train takes us back to Luton, we could look across to Holy Trinity Church and make a note to return in the not too distant future to further explore this disappearing part of rural life.

Were there Nuns in Biscot? I can only say that on dark foggy winter's evenings you may still see black hooded figures hurrying along Nunnery Lane responding to the distant ring of a church bell. I was told of nun-like ghostly figures being seen in the front rooms of houses in the Lane. Some residents have now moved.

Colin Cook 2003

A more comprehensive version of this chapter is published in "The Story of Limbury-cum-Biscot".

Chapter 8

The Crawley Family Legacy

*T*he influence of the Crawley family over Luton during the past five centuries has been constant and beneficial to the town. This was most noticeable in the 19th Century when Luton emerged from a rural to an industrial economy, with the resulting increase in population. John Sambrooke Crawley inherited the lands of the estate and house at Stockwood in 1852 and as a prominent member of the Church of England subscribed to the restoration of St Mary's Church and to the building of new churches in the expanding town and the surrounding hamlets. His interest also included education and he was involved in the provision of National (Church of England) schools in the town and also at Biscot and Stopsley. He and his wife Sarah supported the Luton Cottage Hospital and were among its first patrons.

The Crawley family in Luton can be traced back to the 14th Century and had close and continuous links with the town for over five hundred years. This connection was finally broken when the house and estate was purchased by the Borough of Luton in 1945. Today Stockwood Craft Museum is housed in the stable block, which once formed a part of Stockwood House. Only one small two-storeyed part of the original building survives and this can be seen on the south west corner of the museum. *(When*

Colin wrote this in 2003 Stockwood Craft Museum had not yet been redeveloped as Stockwood Discovery Centre.)

The Crawleys have long been associated with Luton, one of the first mentions of them being William Crawley in the Dallow Court Rolls of 1455AD. The Crawleys were the only family in Luton of which it can be said that they owned lands up to the middle of the last century (1950s) which their forefathers had transmitted from father to son.

Many members of the family are mentioned in the Register of the Luton Guild of the Holy Trinity and by the 1580s, no fewer than eight Crawleys were living in or near Luton; they were farmers, landowners and maltsters, and steadily accumulated property throughout this period. By gradually extending and consolidating their holdings, the Crawleys had become one of the principal land-owning families in Bedfordshire in the early 18th Century. *(Luton Museum Information Sheet No 9.)*

The origin of the family name is interesting, for it was not until the reign of Edward I (1272-1307) that the adoption of surnames was encouraged, to simplify legal registrations regarding the transfer of land and property. King Edward directed that people might take as a name the town or place of their birth. The Crawley family followed the fashion, and took their surname from the place of their birth and the property they owned at "Crawley" in Luton.

Crawley was originally written as "Craulea" and is compounded of two words, "Crau" signifying a hill or crag, and "lea" or "ley" an open clearing in a wood for the pasture of cattle. Crawley Green stands on a hill and in the past it adjoined a wood which covered the upper part of Hart Hill, while on the other side was Spittlesea Wood. Until the expansion of Luton, Crawley Green and Nether Crawley were the names of farms belonging to the Crawley family.

The site of Crawley Green is at the top of the hill on the road leading from Luton to Cockernhoe. Crawley Green and

St Ann's Hill lie to the right of the road and Hart Hill to the left. Cowridge End refers to the land stretching from Crawley Green along the top of Hart Hill to Round Green. If we continue along the road to Cockernhoe we come to "Nether Crawley", lying at the foot of the hill beyond Crawley Green. The word Nether signifies lower, and Nether Crawley was obviously so named to distinguish it from Crawley on the top of the hill. At Nether Crawley we are surrounded on all sides by Crawley property - Crawley Green, Eaton Green, Faulkners Hall, Wigmore Hall, Haverings, Lammers, Lane Farm, Cowridge End and Ramridge End.

In St Mary's Church just outside of the Wenlock Chapel there lays a large black marble gravestone on which is carved a shield bearing three storks; under is written as follows -

"Here ly buried the bodys of Thomas Crawley of Nether Crawley in the parish of Luton, in the co Bedford, Gent., who died 15 Dec.1629. And of Sir Francis Crawley Kt. one of the Judges of the Common Pleas (son and heir of the said Thomas Crawley) who died 13 Feb 1649. And of Francis Crawley (son and heir of the said Sir Francis Crawley) one of the Barons of the Exchequer, who died 25 Feb 1682."

Sir Francis bought Someries from the Rotherham family in the same year that his father died, and with it the right of burial in Someries (Wenlock) Chapel. From the records only the above three Crawleys were buried in the Chapel.

In 1533 a certain George Rotherham obtained from Queen Mary letters of patent authorising him to purchase amongst others the following properties: the farm and the chapel of Farley with the Manors of Farley and Wyperley in Luton, Bedfordshire. The Farley and Wyperley Estate comprised of between five and six hundred acres, and continued in the possession of the Farley Rotherhams until the year 1708. Thomas Rotherham had no son, which was probably the reason for selling in 1708 to Richard Crawley a fair portion of his land. Stockwood, alias

Wyperley, lay on one side of the road from Luton to Caddington and the Farley land on the opposite side. The property sold to Richard Crawley was: Stockwood alias Wyperley, together with the Newlands Fields, bordering Newlands Road and the Lawn (where we get the name of the path through the estate). All these names indicate lands within the present Stockwood Park, and also in the direction of Woodside and Slip End. Thomas Rotherham seems to have retained Farley and left it to his wife Elizabeth.

At the time of the Civil War, Luton in common with other major towns in the area favoured the Parliamentary cause, although the land-owning families were for the King. Among these was Frances Crawley who was a lawyer and in 1632 had been made a judge. Before the actual beginning of the war Charles was striving hard to raise money without calling a Parliament together. In 1635 he appointed twelve judges to advise him on the legality of imposing the Ship Money Tax in a time of peace. Frances Crawley was one of the twelve who advised the King that he alone could decide whether the tax was necessary and could impose it on the whole country if he thought fit. The King did as advised and this was to be the spark which led to war. At the beginning of the war Parliamentary troops were stationed at Someries to watch the Crawleys. After the execution of the King in 1649 the Crawleys had their estates returned to them on the payment of large fines.

From 1728 to 1740 Mr John Crawley made further purchases of property including 50 acres of land and a farm house at Cowridge End and a farm at Farley abutting on to Farley Green.

In 1724 John Crawley sold the Someries estate to Sir John Napier. The Crawley home before 1740 had been "Haverings", which was a large mansion, the foundations of which could be traced until the land was taken over by the expansion of Luton Airport. Mr Crawley wanted a more imposing property for his familly seat and decided to build a new home at Stockwood.

While the new house was being built he lived for a time in London and then at Harpenden. It would appear that living at Harpenden Mr Crawley could direct the laying out of the park at Stockwood and superintend the erection of Stockwood House. The house was completed in 1740 at a cost of £60,000, the year of John Crawley's marriage to Susannah Sambrooke, and this was to become the home of the Crawley family until the middle of the 20th Century. About a century after it was built the house was given a facing of coade stone and red tile which gave it a colourful appearance.

The park is bordered to the north-east by the Farley Road running from Luton to Caddington and Markyate, towards the west by Newlands Road connecting Farley Road with the London Road, and on the south by the London Road. There are Lodges on the Farley Road and Newlands Road. On the London Road there was another smaller Lodge. Between the Farley Road Lodge and the site of the house there is still a fine avenue of chestnut trees. The home farm was situated outside the park on the north side of Farley Road, the farm buildings standing on the site of the ancient hospital of Farley, now part of the Farley Hill Estate.

It is hard to tell whether the house at Stockwood encouraged the wealthy heiress Susannah Sambrooke to live there, or was its building part of the marriage settlement? John Crawley brought to the marriage his vast lands and farms in and around Luton, together with the tithes of Luton, Stockwood and Biscot, with their respective tithe-barns. Susannah brought into the Crawley family the inheritance of an estate in North Bedfordshire consisting of nearly 3,000 acres.

A large establishment was needed to maintain a house and estate of such size and importance as Stockwood. The 1871 Census gives details of those who were living at the house and its lodges. In addition to John S Crawley and his wife Sarah and their six children, there were the following servants: a governess, two nurses and a nurse maid, a butler, a housekeeper, two footmen, four housemaids, a kitchenmaid, a scullery maid, a laundress and three laundry maids, a gardener, two under gardeners and two grooms.

The Park at Stockwood even up to the 1920s was known locally as the "The Lawn". The chief drawback of the Park as a place of residence was that it had a public footpath running from east to west through its entire length, forming a convenient short cut from Luton to the village of Woodside. Originally, up to 1818 the path passed to the south of the house and seriously detracted from the privacy of the grounds and gardens which lie on that side of the house. On 15th August 1817 an order was made by two local justices of the peace for diverting and turning this path to its present position to the north of the mansion. On 5th October 1818 the justices viewed the new footway which was 1,770 yards in length and in breadth 4 feet. To prevent the public from encroaching onto the park, the asphalt path was metal fenced on either side. I remember family Sunday walks along this path with my sister in her the pram, and how difficult it was when passing other families.

John Sambrooke Crawley, who was born 29th April 1823, was throughout his life a generous benefactor to the Church of England in Luton and the surrounding area: this was most welcome as it came at a time of great expansion in church building among other facilities to meet the rapid rise in population. Apart from the restoration of the chancel at St Mary's, he contributed to the erection and endowment of the church at East Hyde and to Christ Church, St Matthew's, St Paul's, St Andrew's, St Saviour's and St Thomas' Stopsley.

Mr J S Crawley was Lord of the Manor of Biscot and responsible for providing the land and for the erection of the church and vicarage (now demolished) and the stables (now the church hall) of Holy Trinity Biscot in 1868. Holy Trinity Church Biscot together with St Andrews at Woodside were planned and built by Mr J S Crawley and are pure examples of his influence. Inside Biscot church is a plaque to his memory and beneficence. On the front of the pulpit is a bust reputed to be of Squire Crawley's head, keeping watch for those sleeping through the sermon. There is also a plaque to the memory of Marina Crawley, second wife of Samuel Crawley, John's father.

John Crawley's interests extended to the education and health of the town contributing to the National (Church of England) schools at Queen's Square, Christ Church, St Matthew's and New Town School (the building is now St Paul's Church) and in 1855 establishing a small National Day School for 50 children at Biscot. He also erected at his own expense a National school at Stopsley for the accommodation of 200 children; the school measured 50 feet by 20 feet, with a neat building attached for the master. Mr Crawley served as a J P in Luton and as the local

The Pulpit at Holy Trinity Church, Biscot,
showing Squire Crawley's head

Conservative Party Chairman. He was also an M P for Honiton, a pocket borough in Devon.

The New Bedford Road was opened in 1832; its construction cut across the Great Moor and along its east side a number of large villas were built for some of Luton's leading industrialists. A handful of these, such as the Leaside and Rookwood, are still standing. The coming of the railway to Luton in 1867 involved building the line across the Great Moor which depleted it still further, and although initially in 1844 objectors had prevented the line being built, this time objectors were few; the prospect of a direct line to London, the Midlands and the North outweighed any other consideration. The southern part of the Moor now cut off by the railway was taken over by J S Crawley with the money which the railway company had given in compensation for part of the Moor needed for the railway itself. In exchange he gave the town the huge open spaces between Old Bedford Road and High Town, which we now know as Pope's Meadow, People's Park and Bells Close. The portions Mr Crawley had taken were developed for the building of Crawley Road, Moor Street and Francis Street.

Mr and Mrs J S Crawley gave financial support to the building of the Luton Cottage Hospital in High Town Road, which opened in 1872. The Cottage Hospital was replaced by the Bute Hospital in Dunstable Road in 1882 to meet the town's growing needs, and from 1887 to 1896 Mr John S Crawley was the President of the Committee of Management. His son Francis Crawley was President from 1897 to 1914. It is interesting to note that in 1873 one of the committee members of the Cottage Hospital was the Rev E R Adams, Vicar of Biscot.

Luton's first Cottage Hospital (1872-1882) had been founded by Dr Edward Woakes, Medical Officer of the Board of Health. A nucleus of money was essential to the enterprise and this was readily obtained from the local landed gentry, led by Mrs Crawley of Stockwood. An old cottage, one of a pair, was rented in High

Town Road at the top of Duke Street on the site now occupied by the High Town Methodist Church, for an annual sum of £25. The cottage was furnished for £48 and opened on 6th May 1872 as the Luton Cottage Hospital. There were originally three beds but within a short time a fourth bed became necessary. All that is left now is a small grass area at the rear of the church once part of the hospital garden. From a report in 1876, eight beds were then in regular use plus an extra in an emergency. The trained nurse was paid £30 per year (Bedfordshire Archives). The hospital was provided for the Artisan class of patient. The rich went to hospitals in London and the poor to the workhouse infirmary, which was mainly for the old and infirm and for girls in trouble. Bute Hospital, which opened in 1882, had 20 beds rising to 27. The cost of both hospitals and later the L&D were raised by public subscription. Hospital Saturday street and factory collections reached £484, the Bute (St Mary's) Hospital cost over £4,000 (Mates book on Luton).

After the 1st World War Miss Joan Crawley (later Mrs Ross-Skinner), who was one of the surviving members of the family which had so long an association with Luton, gave the town the fine stretch of hills off Dallow Road known as the Downs.

Lt and Mrs Ross-Skinner, the last members of the Crawley family to live at Stockwood, left at the beginning of the Second World War, intimating that they did not intend to live at Stockwood after the war. In the usual course of events this would have signalled the decline of this imposing mansion through neglect, vandalism and eventual demolition. However, a new role was being planned for the house and grounds.

During the 2nd World War the hospitals in Luton had links with St Bartholomew's (Barts) Hospital in London. Barts had an annexe for children with orthopaedic problems at Swanley, Kent, "The Queen Alexandra Hospital". The site was close enough to a railway junction and factories to make it an unsafe location for children and at the outbreak of war arrangements were made to transfer the hospital, staff, children and all to the safety of Stockwood. There was a close, happy atmosphere between children and staff and the people of Luton in this rural environment. Many children were now too far away for parents to visit and caring Lutonians filled this gap by regular visits. The house continued to be used as a hospital until 1958.

In 1945 the Town Council bought Stockwood from the Ross-Skinners (purchase price £100,000), which broke the long connection of the Crawley family with the town. Although the house had been used as a hospital during the war and up to 1958, it was not possible to find another useful purpose for it and so regrettably this once stately home was demolished in 1964.

Although the house was demolished, the stable block and walled gardens were retained. At first the stables were used for storage, but in 1974 a plan was put forward to convert and develop them as a museum, a plan which eventually came to fruition on 12th July 1986, when Stockwood Craft Museum and Gardens were officially opened by Mrs Ross-Skinner, the last member of the Crawley family to live at Stockwood House.

The majority of the items on display in the Craft Museum were collected by Thomas Bagshawe whose family owned an engineering factory in Dunstable. He had a lifetime interest in the crafts of Bedfordshire and from 1927 had assembled one of the finest collections of rural trade items in the country. Today we can all benefit from his foresight and collecting instinct.

The Walled Garden and Pleasure Gardens that now form part of the Craft Museum complex were once an integral part of Stockwood House. The Walled Garden provided out of season fruit and vegetables and shelter and warmth for fruit trees to grow comfortably against the mellow brick walls or to be planted in the shade of a north or east facing wall to hold back growth.

Today the grounds are a public park, incorporating a fine rural museum housed in the original stable complex and walled gardens, a restaurant, a golf course, a running track and rugby pitches. It also houses the impressive Mossman Collection. Beyond the garden walls is a landscape garden inspired by the classical style of the 18th Century complete with a Ha-Ha and sculptural works created by Ian Hamilton Finlay.

Please enjoy this fine park and give a thought to the Crawleys who made it all possible.

Postscript : Stockwood

The story of Stockwood goes back to the reign of Henry II (1154-1189). The King, as you would expect, owned large tracts of land throughout England and was Lord of the Manor of Luton. Henry spent most of his life in France and when he was waiting for a boat to England stayed in the Hospital of the Trinity (a resting place for travellers; from the word Hospital we get the word Hospitality) near Calais, run by the monks of a nearby hamlet called Wissant. He must have enjoyed his stay because in 1156 he gave the monks some of the land of the Manor of Luton to enable them to build a hospital and chapel on Farley Hill. The building stood in Farley Farm Road, its lands comprising all of the now Farley Farm Estate and Stockwood Park (then known as Wyperley).

William Wenlock held the post of Hospital Master towards the end of the 14th Century, and in his will gave directions that

Stockwood House

he should be buried in Luton Church (his tomb is in the Wenlock Chapel). In the mid 15th Century George Rotherham obtained the lease on the Hospital, farm and manor of Farley and in 1522 was paying rent to Henry VIII. On Henry's death his son Edward gave the property to one of his knights, but when Mary came to the throne she restored it to the Rotherham family.

After completion of the Park and Mansion House in 1740 the whole estate was given the more dignified name of Stockwood.

The Descendants of William Crawley and Alice Attewelle

William Crawley married Alice Attewelle about 1455

William Crawley about 1466

Thomas Crawley about 1511

John Crawley of Nether Crawley died 1544

Richard Crawley of Nether Crawley died 1578

Thomas Crawley of Nether Crawley died 1629 / married Dorothy Edgerley

Sir Francis Crawley (Judge of Common Pleas) died 1649 / married Elizabeth Rotherham

Sir Francis Crawley (Cursitor Baron of the Exchequer) died 1683 / married Mary Clutterbuck

John Crawley (Councillor at Law) died 1694

Richard Crawley (Register of Admiralty) purchased Stockwood 1708 / married Sarah Dashwood

John Crawley of Stockwood died 1767, built house at Stockwood 1740 / married Susanna Sambrooke

John Crawley of Stockwood born 1743, died 1815 / married Elizabeth Hawley

Samuel Crawley of Stockwood died 1852 / married Theodosia Mary Vyner (1st wife) Maria Musgrave (2nd wife)

John Sambrook Crawley of Stockwood born 1823, died 1895 / married Sarah Bridget Wells

Francis Crawley of Stockwood born 1853 / married Edith Rosa Ferguson

Joan Crawley last of Crawleys at Stockwood born 1900, later Mrs J Crawley-Ross-Skinner

Colin Cook 2003

Appendix

Colin enjoyed writing his own poems in the style of the Odd Odes narrated by the late Cyril Fletcher. He wrote some for Holy Trinity Church, Biscot, and recited them at their Harvest Suppers. Two are included in this book.

The Tale of Frederick Napp

This is the tale of Frederick Napp,
who thought himself a clever chap,
growing prize marrows was his scene,
and to gain first prize was his dream,
a gigantic vegetable he would grow
for the annual Flower Show.
Fred's marrow was nursed both day and night,
kept from greenfly, bugs and blight,
fertilized until it could take no more,
all love and tenderness our lad did pour,
until the eve of the Flower Show,
when fate dealt our hero a vicious blow.

The marrow rested beneath a pane of glass,
upon which a pussy cat happened to pass.
Its progress was seen by our enraged Fred,
who aimed a house brick at the pussy's head.
The brick smashed glass and veg asunder
and the poor lad realized his dreadful blunder.
"What have I done?" was Fred's anguished moan,

as pussy quickly made tracks for home.

Now Fred's not a man to sit and mope,
and of his dreams he still had hope,
perhaps a balloon of similar shape and size
as a marrow he could disguise.
So it came to pass at the Flower Show,
everyone gasped, though none could know.
At the first prize marrow females did swoon,
little realising it was an air filled balloon.

Fred was elated, a winner at last,
when along came the Vicar and boldly did ask,
"that marrow Fred" and tapped his napper,
"we'll eat it at the Harvest Supper".
Fred could only stand and stare
while the Vicar departed with balloon and air.

To the Harvest Supper came one and all,
and for Fred his greatest fall.
"Be careful with my marrow" he did implore,
as it went into the oven on regulo four.
Everyone said "that marrow will taste grand",
but in the oven the veg started to expand,
until the balloon could stand no more,
and exploded through the oven door.

The force stripped Fred of every stitch
and deposited him through the window niche.
He there stuck fast with feet a'kicking
and everyone came into the kitchen
to see the unusual scene,
a naked Fred caught by a beam.
The vicar drew himself up to a dignified height

and said "who has seen such a dreadful sight?"
"I have," said his wife unashamed,
"often, but never framed."

Colin Cook early 1980s

The Tale of Sonya Snell

This is the tale of Sonya Snell,
to whom an accident befell.
It happened down at her local,
I don't mean Inn, but Holy Parochial.

Harvest Festival was the order of the day,
and along went Sonya all spruced up and gay,
her annual visit with all to share,
to make sure Vicar and Church were still there.
As the service started she cried "Oh dearie me,
They have finished with Two and are on Series Three.
What's happened to Thee and Thou and Art,
and all the people taking part?"

But when the old harvest hymns were sung,
Sonya, with the all the rest, was won.
After the sermon, the Vicar did declare
to all the souls who had gathered there,
"Now is the time to hand in your loot,
I'm sorry, I mean your baskets of fruit."
The congregation then, in two's and one's,
handed over apples, pears and plums.
They even offered bottles of liqueur
to the old Sexton and the Vicar.

Sonya, of course, joined in with the rest,
offering nothing but the best.
Eggs and tomatoes formed the main part,
as down the nave on her way she did start,
with head held high, as in marble halls,
she swept regally past the choir stalls.
And there was made a mistake most grave,
because in a choir there's always one knave,
a little lad, angelic looking maybe,
but who hits on any chance he can see.

In this instance the little lad was Jim,
about to dispose of a banana skin.
The banana he had consumed away,
when for all the rest it was heads down and pray.
Sonya was his victim, fate could not deny,
as under her feet, the skin he did shy.
The Sexton, his hands outstretched before,
didn't know for what he was in store,
as eggs and tomatoes came his way,
and poor Sonya in the chancel did lay.

Our Sexton, not wishing this fate to meet,
stepped smartly back onto the Vicar's feet,
and there they stood, in passionate embrace,
with eggs and tomatoes on either face.
The words then uttered, the noo,
cannot be found in series Three or Two.
But the moral drawn is surely sound,
when placing feet upon the ground,
do not be proud with head held high,
or like Sonya, you could fly.

Colin Cook early 1980s

128